CHATHAM HO

PREDICAMENT

CHATHAM HOUSE PAPERS

General Series Editor: William Wallace
Soviet Foreign Policy Programme Director: Alex Pravda

Chatham House Papers are short monographs on current policy problems which have been commissioned by the Royal Institute of International Affairs. In preparing the paper, authors are advised by a study group of experts convened by the RIIA. Publication of the paper by the Institute indicates its standing as an authoritative contribution to the public debate.

The Royal Institute of International Affairs is an independent body which promotes the rigorous study of international questions and does not express opinions of its own. The opinions expressed in this publication are the responsibility of the author.

CHATHAM HOUSE PAPERS · 37

THE NUCLEAR PREDICAMENT

EXPLORATIONS IN SOVIET IDEOLOGY

Stephen Shenfield

The Royal Institute of International Affairs

Routledge & Kegan Paul
London, New York and Andover

First published 1987
by Routledge & Kegan Paul Ltd
11 New Fetter Lane, London EC4P 4EE
29 West 35th Street, New York, NY 10001, USA, and
North Way, Andover, Hants SP10 5BE

Reproduced from copy supplied by
Stephen Austin and Sons Ltd and
printed in Great Britain by
Redwood Burn Limited
Trowbridge, Wiltshire

ISBN 0-7102-1228-3

CONTENTS

ACKNOWLEDGMENTS

I should like to thank all those at Chatham House who have helped with this study: in particular William Wallace for persuading me to write it; Alex Pravda for his encouragement and for including the study within the Chatham House Soviet foreign policy programme funded by the ESRC; Pauline Wickham for her work as editor; and Lolli Duvivier and Marie Lathia for their word-processing labours. Thank you also to all those, particularly members of the Chatham House study group, who have commented on the drafts or discussed the subject-matter with me.

The financial support of my work by the MacArthur Foundation is gratefully acknowledged.

S.D.S.

1

INTRODUCTION

'Peace' and 'socialism' are the two most salient values in the Soviet ideology of international affairs. The problem of relating the one to the other in the nuclear age is the focus of this study.

For Lenin as for Marx, worldwide 'socialism' or 'communism' was the supreme, absolute value and goal. Efficacy in advancing it was the sole criterion by which action was to be judged. Eventual attainment of the goal was guaranteed by the laws of history.

In the earliest years of the Soviet State, the Bolsheviks were tempted by the hope that socialist revolution abroad might be catalysed by a strategy of revolutionary war. Defeat in the war with Poland in 1920 and the subsiding of the revolutionary wave in Europe led to this hope being abandoned. Instead, 'peace' was enshrined as a vital value, though a relative one subsidiary to 'socialism'. For the weak Soviet Union to become embroiled in large-scale war with other great powers would be the greatest threat to the security of the Soviet State, and thus to the cause of which the USSR was the self-appointed bastion. The need for peace motivated all the manoeuvres of prewar Soviet diplomacy.

Military inferiority no longer dictates the need for peace as it did in the past. But it has been replaced by an even stronger motive – the fear of nuclear devastation. How can the ship of history be steered past the nuclear rocks to the safe port of communism?

Ideology and Soviet foreign policy

In the USSR, social and political issues are systematically analysed, at least in official meetings and publications, within the compulsory constraints of the conceptual framework and core assumptions of what is known as 'Marxism-Leninism'. This activity, which is called 'ideology', enjoys a prominent status in the power apparatus, and is the concern of a whole stratum of officials, scholars and publicists.

In the absence of a revolutionary transformation of the Soviet system, one cannot expect change in the core assumptions, such as the tendency of society to develop towards world communism. However, post-Stalinist Soviet ideology is not static or monolithic: there is room for divergent tendencies to emerge and compete for dominance. Even in periods like the middle and late 1970s, when a high degree of uniformity was imposed, some significant variation could be observed. Under Gorbachev, variation has reached in important areas the level of relatively open debate. Debate remains, of course, the privilege of a narrow elite, and proceeds in accordance with established conventions (for example, the identity of the opponent is rarely made explicit). This is dictated by a political system which Dmitri Simes has described as 'controlled elite pluralism within carefully defined totalitarian limits'.[1]

Who does take part in ideological debate? At the top, we have Secretaries of the Central Committee and officials in relevant departments of the Central Committee apparatus (e.g. the International Department, the Propaganda Department). We shall be meeting people of this kind later: Dobrynin, Yakovlev, Zagladin, Shakhnazarov, etc. (Biographical data on the most important ideologists cited are given in the Glossary.) Next there are other occupants of high Party positions – for instance, the Pro-Rector of the Academy of Social Sciences, the Central Committee think-tank (Krasin); editors of the theoretical Party journal *Kommunist* (Kosolapov, Frolov); and consultants attached to Central Committee departments (e.g. Zhilin).

At a less authoritative level, the most prominent members of such professional groups as economists, sociologists, philosophers, foreign-affairs analysts, diplomats and military strategists also contribute to ideological debate. This includes the directors of such institutes of the Academy of Sciences as the Institute for the Study of the USA and Canada (G. Arbatov), the Institute of World Economy and International Relations (Primakov) and the Institute of the International Workers' Movement (Timofeyev). A role is played, finally, by a few influential publicists such as *Izvestiya* commentator Alexander Bovin and *Literary Gazette* observer Fedor Burlatsky.

Both the closeness and the direction of the connection between ideology and policy-making have long been matters of controversy.[2] Does ideology merely serve to legitimize policies that are really motivated by quite extraneous considerations, perhaps by a traditional conception of Russian national interest or by a thirst for power for its own sake? Or is it, as it proclaims itself to be, a guide to action?

The evidence suggests that any simple answer would be misleading. A high-ranking defector describes both a cynically instrumental approach to ideology on the part of senior officials and the deep impact of ideology on their perceptions.[3] For one person, ideology may be just a game that has to be played, while for a second person it may be a means of understanding the world and for a third a bit of both.

The institutional role of ideology also changes over time. Under Stalin the job of ideologists was simply to work out *post hoc* justifications for the leaders' policy choices. But as ideology has become a larger-scale, more complex and specialized activity, it has acquired a limited autonomy. It is still subject to very strong influence from above, as ideologists seek patronage by adapting their output to the perceived needs of the leadership, but leaders are less able or inclined to exert direct and detailed control. There is some scope for ideologists to propose concepts and arguments of their own which may win endorsement: they may influence the leaders as well as be influenced by them. This is especially true during those periods like the present when a new leadership is in the process of formulating its positions.

The closeness of the link between policy and ideological debate varies enormously according to subject area, situation and the personalities involved. At one extreme, prominent ideologists known to be close to the leadership may be analysing matters which have a clear and immediate bearing on policy decisions. At the other, obscure scholars may be arguing at a level of abstraction so rarified that any significant link with policy is unlikely. On the whole, the link between ideology and policy cannot be very tight, because ideology by its nature deals with general concepts (such as relations between socialism and capitalism in a given historical period), whereas policy must concern itself with specifics (such as relations between the USSR and France at a certain point in time). For this among other reasons, one would not expect any clear correspondence between ideological tendencies and factional groupings within the leadership stratum.

Ideology and 'real' views

If only for convenience, one tends to refer to ideas published under the name of a Soviet ideologist as his 'views'. But the relationship between published ideas and 'real views', if any, is a very controversial matter.

We need to distinguish two questions here. One is the relationship between published ideas and personal views as expressed in private conversation with trusted friends. Of greater direct importance is the relationship between published ideas and the 'real official views' which guide secret policy deliberations in the Politburo, the International Department of the Central Committee and other official bodies. It is of course extremely difficult to judge these matters from the outside, though arbitrary speculations based on one or another set of prejudices are hardly in short supply.

The scope for the expression of personal views depends on the position which a writer occupies as well as the ideological acceptability of his personal views. A Party official, for instance, is much more constrained by his official position than an influential publicist like Bovin or Burlatsky who enjoys status of a more informal kind. Even in the best of cases, editing, censorship and self-censorship will prevent the *full* expression of personal views, which is why we have to read between the lines for hidden meanings and implications. Similarly, the exposition of official views in even the most authoritative of Party documents is no doubt incomplete, concealing many sensitive matters.

It is often argued that at least some published ideas are not just selective but deliberately false indications of beliefs really held. Three types of argument are commonly put forward:

(a) That certain Soviet statements are no more than *propaganda* designed to manipulate one or another target audience, internal or external. Hard-line Western analysts generally discount the more conciliatory parts of Soviet ideology by attributing them to an effort to disinform Western opinion.

(b) That certain Soviet statements should be regarded as no more than empty *ritual*. It is by this argument that soft-line Western analysts often minimize the significance of the more confrontational parts of Soviet ideology.

(c) That certain Soviet statements are *instruments* used on behalf of different bureaucratic interest groups *in the competition for resources*. For example, what appear to be divergent assessments of the nuclear threat are to be seen as economically motivated bids to divert resources towards or away from the military sector.

There is undoubtedly considerable truth in *all* of these arguments. Statements aimed at Western audiences do put more stress on conciliation with the West, and much less stress on the struggle between the systems, than speeches to Soviet Party audiences.[4] One must be alive to any systematic differences between internally oriented Party material, the most reliable vehicle of official views, and mass propaganda for Soviet and for foreign audiences. Ritual is a strong and openly avowed current in Soviet public life, though now becoming less pervasive under the impact of Gorbachev's campaign against 'formalism'. And bureaucratic rivalry is a feature of permanent importance in Soviet politics.

However, there is a danger of exaggerating these points beyond what the evidence will bear. Thus, while ideas are slanted to different audiences, there remains a great deal of common ground between what is presented to one audience and what is presented to another, and there is significant variety within the material prepared for any given audience.[5] If I had to guess the contents of a Soviet article on a given subject, it would help to know both the name of the author and the name of the journal (as an indicator of the target audience). But if I were allowed to know only one of these two pieces of information, I would choose the name of the author.

The extreme forms of both the 'propaganda' and the 'ritual' arguments reduce to a false uniformity the apparent variety of Soviet views (though they do this in opposite ways). They thereby discount the significance of internal debate, for which there is less evidence than the researcher would like but more than can convincingly be explained away.

To the extent that some ideas might be only propaganda or ritual, it needs still to be borne in mind that even propaganda and ritual have political consequences through their impact on the social atmosphere. The possibility that published ideas may to some extent reflect real views should not then be too readily rejected. One must guard against logically unsound habits of thought in this area. Detecting a propaganda advantage in some Soviet statement does not prove it to be just propaganda, nor is the fact that an idea is incredible to us any reason to think that its espousal by others, accustomed to a different world-view, cannot be sincere.

Words and meanings
In analysing Soviet ideology, one is driven continually to make use of its language. I have not cluttered up the text with distancing quotation marks every time that I borrow a Soviet term, but I would like to stress nevertheless that the terms – and the concepts underlying them – are those imposed by the material under study, not those that I would personally consider adequate to an understanding of the world. For example, I shall refer, following my sources, to 'the socialist countries', but this does not mean that I find this label illuminating in any way.

What Soviet ideological terms might mean to their users is itself a very complicated matter, to which I can allude here only briefly. A general warning is in order that meanings may be complex or ambiguous, varying with the context and over time, and that they often differ in important ways from apparent equivalents in Western political language, though this does not mean that there is no connection whatsoever.

Thus 'communism' refers to the fully developed communal society of the future (a distant future, it is now held), and is never applied to existing communist-ruled States, which are 'socialist'. 'Socialism' may be used in the abstract to refer to a system of social relations, or it may mean the aggregate social force constituted by the socialist countries (e.g. 'the world position of socialism', 'the policy of socialism').

But where are the boundaries in determining which conceivable social systems would qualify as socialist, and which countries form part of world socialism? In the past, 'socialism' meant simply the type of system existing in the USSR, allowing for relatively unimportant national variations, or the Soviet-dominated bloc, so that 'the advance of socialism' could reasonably be understood as equivalent in practice to the expansion of the area under Soviet control. Now that Soviet ideology includes deviant or independent States – Hungary, Romania, Yugoslavia and 'our great neighbour Socialist China' – within a more loosely conceived socialist camp, things are less clear-cut. While in many contexts 'socialism' still seems to bear interpretation purely in terms of the power of the USSR, a new conception of socialist advance has emerged under Andropov and Gorbachev which envisages a long period of differentiation among socialist countries before they ultimately merge into the worldwide composite form of 'integral socialism'.

Guide to the argument

Chapters 2–9 are concerned primarily with the conceptual development of Soviet ideology. Chapters 10–12 are devoted to discussion of the political significance of this development.

The post-Stalinist foreign-policy ideology of the USSR has successively encountered two challenges. First, there has been increasing recognition of the catastrophic consequences of nuclear war (Chapter 2), and this has placed in doubt the inevitability of humanity's communist future (Chapter 3). Second, it was held from the 1950s up to the 1970s that peace would be steadily strengthened as the 'correlation of forces' in the world changed to the advantage of socialism (Chapter 4). This doctrine was undermined by the collapse of detente at the turn of the 1980s.

The coincidence of these two challenges gave rise to a crisis in Soviet ideology, to which there have been a variety of divergent responses. The most radical response, which has become more salient under Gorbachev, shifts the stress from the correlation of forces to growing international interdependence as the crucial material factor working in favour of detente (Chapter 5).

We explore various aspects of the contrast between the new tendency and the orthodoxy it is tending to supplant. Elevation of the status of 'peace' as a social value indicates an inclination towards greater restraint in foreign policy (Chapter 6). Reassessment of the relationship between capitalism and militarism leads to a more optimistic stance on the attainability of a stable peace between the two systems (Chapter 7). Interdependence, according to the new approach, necessitates worldwide cooperation to achieve security, to tackle other global problems and to develop the world economy (Chapter 8). The new tendency does not completely supersede reliance upon the correlation of forces, but it does attach increased weight to the non-military dimensions of the correlation (Chapter 9).

The current political strength of the various ideological tendencies is compared, and it is shown that the new tendency, though now very influential, does not yet possess uncontested dominance (Chapter 10). The extent to which the new tendency finds its reflection in current policy in the fields of arms control, trade and international cooperation is very briefly considered (Chapter 11). Finally, the implications for the West are discussed. The conclusion is drawn that a new Soviet strategy requires an appropriate strategy of response from the West (Chapter 12).

2

THE CONSEQUENCES OF NUCLEAR WAR

The development of the Soviet position

It is openly stated by Soviet commentators that the Soviet view of nuclear war has changed. 'It took time', says Gorbachev, 'for our society and the Soviet leadership to develop an interest in the new mode of thinking. We pondered a good deal . . . before we saw things as they are. . . . We made ourselves realize that . . . the human race has lost its immortality.'[1] Let us glance back at 'the prolonged process of maturation'[2] of the current official position that there would be neither victors nor vanquished in nuclear war.[3]

Stalin denied that any weapon could change the basic nature of war as a social phenomenon. Following Stalin's death, there was an attempt by the new prime minister, Malenkov, and some other officials to establish the opposite line, whereby a new world war was identified with 'the destruction of world civilization'.[4] The idea recurred in the Soviet media during the first quarter of 1954 and then again disappeared from view. Malenkov was removed in early 1955. An editorial in the Party's theoretical journal, *Kommunist*, then denounced the thesis of the destruction of civilization as a lie invented by the capitalist enemy in order to demoralize the masses and intimidate those Soviet-bloc politicians 'weak-nerved and unstable' enough to fall for it.[5]

Nevertheless, the terrible consequences of nuclear war gained increasing official recognition through the late 1950s and early

9

1960s. While at the beginning of the Khrushchev period no qualitative distinction was recognized between the (admittedly vast) devastation of the Second World War and the likely results of a Third, by 1963 the Soviet government was to declare that 'all countries . . . will be thrown back in their development by decades, even centuries'.[6] The polemics against Maoist China, in particular, had helped to catalyse this shift. Yet those who tried to push the development to its limit by rehabilitating Malenkov's position did not succeed. The prospect of survival and 'victory' was not repudiated.

A further shift in the position of the leadership occurred in the early 1970s. Brezhnev, who in 1967 had given notice that 'in combat against any aggressor the Soviet Union will win a victory worthy of our great nation',[7] from 1973 onwards spoke of nuclear war as a danger threatening all humanity.[8]

This change can be linked to the culmination of efforts by various natural and social scientists, journalists and diplomats to arouse doubts concerning the continued validity of traditional military doctrine in the nuclear age. Since 1960 there had been some scope for coded debate on such issues in the press. For example, in 1968 A. Krylov called upon his fellow social and natural scientists to take part in the analysis of strategic questions and to work out a 'strategy for peace'. He criticized 'subjectivists' who 'reject the data of contemporary science concerning the problem of nuclear war'.[9] This provoked an irritated response from one of the 'subjectivists', Maj.-Gen. Bochkarev, who objected that denial of the possibility of attaining victory reduced military strategy and training to absurdity.[10] We also have émigré testimony of the impact made at the highest level of power by studies of nuclear war conducted by the Military Department of the Soviet Sociological Association in the late 1960s and early 1970s.[11]

However, close examination of high-level Soviet statements made in the 1970s reveals that only the possibility, and not the certainty, of nuclear war destroying civilization had been granted. The expressions used were probabilistic in nature (nuclear war 'may destroy', 'threatens the existence of humanity', 'puts the future of civilization at stake'). There was no contradiction between 'political' statements that drew attention to the possibility of total destruction and 'military' statements of the same period that focused on the complementary possibility of 'victory', such as Marshal Ogarkov's article on 'military strategy' in the *Soviet Military Encyclopedia* (1979).[12]

The dominant Soviet outlook was probably reflected in correspondence between Academician Fedoseyev, Vice-President of the Academy of Sciences, and the American philosopher John Somerville in 1974. Even if the USSR were the victim of a first nuclear strike, asked Somerville, how could nuclear retaliation be justified, when it would merely complete the annihilation of mankind? Fedoseyev replied that the annihilation of mankind 'is not the only possible outcome'; it might be possible to achieve the 'decisive destruction of the aggressor's nuclear installations' before this point.[13]

In the 1980s, a further evolution of the official position has occurred. New formulations exclude even the possibility of victory in nuclear war. The undertaking not to use nuclear weapons first was justified by Minister of Defence Marshal Ustinov in 1982 on grounds of 'the impossibility of coming out on top in nuclear conflict'.[14] The view that 'there would be neither victors nor vanquished' in a nuclear war has been incorporated into the new (1986) Party Programme; the old (1969) Party Programme, often quoted by military writers, had merely observed that there would be hundreds of millions of casualties.[15]

Gorbachev has gone so far as to argue, in recognition of the 'nuclear winter' findings, that a nuclear attacker would be committing suicide as a result 'not even of the counterstrike, but of the consequences of the explosion of his own warheads'.[16] He has admitted to some uncertainty regarding whether nuclear war would destroy or merely 'degrade' mankind, the former being 'the most likely result'.[17]

However, the possibility of victory remains implicit in military writings, for example about improving the survivability of the economy,[18] even though the word 'victory' now tends to be avoided in favour of such euphemisms as 'success'. Allusion is occasionally made to continuing resistance to the new line on nuclear war. Thus Trofimenko (of the USA Institute) upbraids unidentified recalcitrants in the name of the leadership: '"Whether we like one another or not, we can survive or perish only together," says M.S. Gorbachev . . . This is not so simple to grasp. What is simpler than to resort to the cliché that only capitalism will perish and socialism will remain? But the Soviet leadership looks the truth in the eyes . . .'[19]

A thread of uncertainty runs through the current Soviet debate. Perhaps the key underlying issue is how, given the uncertainty, to choose assumptions on which to base policy. The publicist Alexander Bovin argues: 'When one takes the price of error into account, it is more expedient in this case to take the worse variant as the truth. This will help us assess anew many customary conceptions, and choose accordingly the saving line of conduct. Choice of the 'better' variant may indeed ... have a provocative effect.'[20]

The meaning of 'victory'

What do Soviet military men and others who conceive of 'victory' in nuclear war have in mind? They entertain no illusions of triumph or glory. They have recognized that a terrible price would be paid – 'a large part of the world's productive forces' destroyed, 'decades, even centuries' needed 'to rebuild the economy, culture and local resources', and the movement towards communism greatly retarded.[21] 'Victory' is won if the Soviet system manages to survive in a recognizable form, and if at the same time the capitalist system collapses. A crucial role is assigned here to expected uprisings of survivors in the capitalist countries against the system that they finally understand to be the source of war. 'We know war is a teacher,' says Admiral Shelyag.[22]

The contrasting political results which constitute victory follow less from any vast difference in the extent of devastation on the two sides than from the moral, political and organizational superiority of the Soviet side. Soviet society is more united, Soviet patterns of organization are better suited to extreme conditions, and Soviet people are more disciplined and loyal, tougher and capable of greater endurance than Westerners. Given the approximately equal quality and quantity of armaments on each side, two military analysts recently argued, the most fruitful goal for Soviet research might be to 'enhance the moral-political superiority of our people', including the 'weakening of the moral potential of the adversary through the system of foreign-policy propaganda'.[23]

In defending the idea of victory in nuclear war, military writers have used three kinds of argument:

(a) Victory is guaranteed by the laws of history, for the imperialists 'are in no position to strike back with their nuclear weapons against the immutable course of historical development, which leads inevitably to the victory of socialism and communism'.[24]

(b)   Confidence in victory is needed to sustain the morale, in peacetime training and in war, of the people and of the armed forces. The morale of troops cannot be strengthened 'on the basis of their recognition of the hopelessness of the struggle for which they are preparing'.[25]

(c)   Practical reasons exist for thinking that victory might be achieved.

Now, while the first and second kinds of arguments require complete exclusion of the prospect of the destruction of civilization, practical arguments are compatible with the possibility of this outcome, provided that the alternative possibility of victory is not excluded. Thus Lieut.-Col. Rybkin has expressed the hope that 'a rapid victory over the aggressor may be achieved which would avert further destruction and calamities'[26] – that is, before the whole enemy nuclear arsenal can be used. Such calculations are, of course, a matter of probabilities, not certainties.[27]

There is therefore some flexibility inherent in the likely stance of practically oriented military professionals on the General Staff, if not in that of the specialists in ideology and morale in the Main Political Administration of the armed forces.

Even so, the military professional finds it difficult to reconcile himself to the notion that in certain circumstances his skills may be useless or counterproductive. Faced with this disconcerting thought, the Soviet military man may take refuge in a form of double-think which holds that political and military thinking express different truths, each valid in its own domain. One 'propagandist' is reported as opening a speech with the words: 'Scientists say that nuclear war cannot be won, but let us proceed from a different assumption.'[28] A retired colonel, interviewed in 1984, explained the discrepancy between the treatment of nuclear war in political and military literature as follows:

All of us, more or less, know that nuclear war would be the end. All our theoreticians say that there is no way of preventing nuclear war from escalating to the global level, that you cannot win a nuclear war. That is our general-theoretical position. But from a professional military point of view such a position is impossible. Nuclear war is conceivable, and a professional military man must consider what to do in that event . . . Just as a

13

doctor, knowing that his patient is suffering from an incurable disease, cannot for that reason abandon further efforts.[29]

The main practical reason for thinking victory attainable is the prospect that war may be brought to an end before the whole of the adversaries' nuclear arsenals are used – either through rapid success in decapitating the enemy's forces, or by limiting the use of nuclear weapons to some regional theatre. Statements by military writers that the 'massive use' of nuclear weapons 'may entail catastrophic consequences for both sides'[30] might be read as implying that *limited* nuclear war is feasible and winnable.

It is true that Soviet commentators often attack notions of limited nuclear war as unrealistic. However, the ridicule is primarily directed at Western theories in which escalation is finely adjusted by bargaining. Nuclear war cannot be 'dosaged' or waged like a duel in accordance with 'gentlemen's rules'.[31] This does not rule out decisive action in pursuit of limited military goals. Moreover, 'the most conclusive and resolute course of action' is called for by a nuclear attack on the USSR itself,[32] leaving open the possibility of a nuclear war restricted to non-Soviet Europe. In 1972 Brezhnev tried to secure this option by seeking an agreement between the USSR and the USA not to use nuclear weapons against one another's territory in the event of war in Europe.[33] Another contingency might be a Soviet-Chinese nuclear war in which the European part of the USSR escapes attack. Soviet strategists have considered escalation from theatre to general nuclear war likely but not inevitable.[34]

A recent shift towards rejecting the feasibility of limited nuclear war may be signalled by Gorbachev's readiness to give up the SS-20 force, the putative tool of theatre nuclear war against Europe and China, in a zero-option INF agreement. This would be consistent with the current adoption of a military strategy relying, if at all possible, on conventional warfare.[35]

Assessment

The assessment of Soviet views on nuclear war must reckon with a range of imponderables – the uncertainty and double-think of Soviet minds, the state of internal controversies, the possible distortion of statements for purposes of external and internal propaganda.

Many Western analysts still hold that Soviet claims to recognize the threat to the existence of civilization posed by nuclear war must be regarded as disinformation designed for external, and possibly internal, audiences. That there has been, and may still be, much deceptive propagandist use of the nuclear-war theme is not disputed. In fact, the practice is noted and deprecated by Soviet writers who argue that what was in the past intended as hyperbole, or an effective oratorical device, has now been 'confirmed by the research of the world's most competent scientists'.[36] However, even if Soviet oratory serves purely as a tool of manipulation, it is less plausible to dismiss as disinformation serious analytical material – for example, the study by a group of Soviet economists, published in 1984, which models mathematically the vulnerability of economic systems to nuclear attack and traces the dynamics of socio-economic regression to barbarism or extinction in the aftermath of nuclear war.[37]

The 'disinformation' hypothesis is, moreover, less credible in explaining internal publicity about the consequences of nuclear war than in accounting for propaganda aimed at the West. The internal publicity has gradually increased to the point where, according to a recent opinion poll, nearly 90 per cent of Soviet people say there could be no victors in nuclear war, with only 4 per cent disagreeing.[38] While the theme may have some advantage as internal propaganda in underlining the peace-loving nature of Soviet policy, this would surely be outweighed for a leadership really hoping for victory in nuclear war by the loss entailed to the 'moral potential' of Soviet survivors. Indeed, Academician Chazov, the top cardiologist (now Minister of Health) who hosted discussions on Soviet television between American and Soviet physicians about the medical conse-quences of nuclear war in June 1982, was criticized by the military for 'demoralizing the Soviet people at a time of great danger'.[39]

We may reasonably conclude that the viewpoint now dominant within the Soviet power elite takes account at least of the possibility of the destruction of civilization in nuclear war. This is the starting-point of the political debate that we are about to examine.

3
THE COMMUNIST GOAL UNDER THREAT

What does the threat of nuclear annihilation mean in the context of the Soviet view of history? What bearing does recognition of the threat have on the central concepts of 'historical inevitability' in general and 'the inevitable victory of socialism and communism' in particular? How did the idea of 'the destruction of civilization' evolve in Marxist tradition, as it is drawn upon by present-day Soviet ideology? To what alternative outlooks on the future may recognition of the nuclear threat in Soviet ideology give rise?

'Inevitability' in the Soviet philosophy of history

Marx and Engels aspired to put socialism upon a 'scientific' basis by demonstrating it to be the result of a historical process subject to 'laws of history' that were analogous to the 'laws of nature', which were themselves conceived of in the nineteenth century in a highly deterministic fashion. Marxist philosophers in the USSR, as elsewhere, argue over the degree to which historical development is predetermined, and over how the founders of Marxism understood the problem. The trend in recent years, again both in the USSR and in the West, has been to adopt within limits a more flexible approach to history, allowing increased scope to chance, and to subjective and other explanatory factors that cannot be regarded as predetermined.

It is convenient to distinguish three viewpoints in these debates. First, there are various dogmatic interpretations of Marxism, including the Stalinist variant, which insist that history is subject to the operation of deterministic laws that can be specified in a fairly detailed way – which social formation follows which, how and under what conditions. This approach is labelled 'mechanical', 'rigid' or 'narrow determinism' by its critics. The middle part of the spectrum is occupied by different kinds of 'broad determinism', which admit the existence of more or less indeterminacy within a framework of broad long-term historical regularities. Finally, as the scope of indeterminacy is expanded, broad determinism merges into a conception of the historical process as essentially 'open' – a conception the Marxist credentials of which are questioned by purists.

The dominant approach in Soviet philosophy nowadays is that of broad determinism. Although (to quote political theorist and Central Committee official Georgy Shakhnazarov) 'we have some primitive theorists who say that only a single line of development is the inevitable one',[1] Soviet writers generally 'presuppose the possibility of different variants within a broadly conceived predetermination'.[2] As explained by the historian G. Ye. Glezerman:

The possibilities for people's action are determined by objective conditions, the level of development of society, etc. But the realization of these possibilities to an enormous degree depends on [people's] consciousness, energy and will ...

At any stage of history there are various, even directly opposed, possibilities. For example, in what forms will the transition be made to a higher type of society? Will a specific revolution win or suffer defeat? The answer to such questions is not uniquely predetermined.[3]

By implication, the most crucial questions, concerning *whether* the transition will be made at all rather than exactly how and when, *do* still have unique answers.

However, some Soviet writers go further, to proclaim 'the openness of history'. According to the philosopher B.T.Grigoryan, 'the course of history is not a track or rut laid down beforehand once and for all. History is not programmed or predetermined by anyone. Historical development is an open system with the broadest possibilities, with an unlimited "set" of probabilities and variations.'[4]

For theories of this kind, historical development can follow a variety of alternative long-term paths, and the orthodox sequence of social formations – primitive communism, slave society, feudalism, capitalism, socialism/communism – is not regarded as compulsory. But while theorizing about pre-industrial societies is unconstrained, the 'inevitability of communism' is much more rarely subjected to any doubt. Thus the Estonian philosopher Eero Loone, who in general stresses the 'multilinearity' of historical development, nevertheless asserts that, 'for a Marxist, one transition is necessary – that from capitalism to communism'.[5]

The inevitability of communism and the nuclear threat

A key argument of those who opposed the thesis of the destruction of civilization in nuclear war always was that, by undermining the inevitability of communism, it 'contradicts the objective laws of history'.[6] 'Weaponry has never abolished the laws of social development,' stated the *Kommunist* editorial against Malenkov in 1955. 'There is and can be no reason to think that atomic weaponry is an exception in this regard.'[7]

A remarkable feature of Soviet ideological literature is that references to the inevitability of communism remain commonplace even now that the possibility of the destruction of civilization in nuclear war is recognized. Shakhnazarov has explained this practice by characterizing nuclear war as an anomalous event outside the purview of Marxism as a social theory, in the same category as a planetary natural catastrophe:

> Of course, when we speak of the inevitable victory of socialism and communism, then we are abstracting from the possibility of all sorts of other events. Let us suppose that some alien body collides with the earth . . . Any general theoretical system must operate within certain limits. It has to assume that the earth will not collide with a cosmic body, that humanity will continue its existence.[8]

This rather artificial expedient of separating the threat of nuclear war from the prospect of normal social development in different ideological compartments serves at least to preserve 'the inevitability of communism' within one of the compartments.

It is against the background of such evasions that one can understand why Grigoryan is so insistent in establishing the equal reality status of the possibility of nuclear war and of the possibility of its prevention:

Humanity now faces two completely real possibilities ... : peace and total disarmament, or nuclear war. ... Progressive philosophical thought and realistic political theory reject various secular and religious variants of the fatalistic ... conception of history and the corresponding fatally pessimistic and fatally optimistic prognoses of the future.[9]

The idea of 'the destruction of civilization'

The idea of the possible destruction of civilization is not new to the nuclear age. Many of the pre-industrial regional civilizations were completely destroyed. This resulted from three types of cause:

(a) natural catastrophe – for example, successive riverine civilizations of the Tigris-Euphrates basin were destroyed by drought and desertification or by flood;

(b) attack by an alien civilization (the Assyrians, Mongols, Conquistadores, etc.); and

(c) internal conflict leading to the breakdown of irrigation facilities, etc.: for example, it is believed that the Old Kingdom of Ancient Egypt collapsed suddenly following a peasant revolt.

It is perhaps the historical memory of the destruction of older civilizations which has helped to keep alive in present-day culture the idea that the contemporary industrial world civilization may also perish from any of these types of cause:

(a) natural catastrophe on a planetary scale – for example, the possible collision of the earth with a cosmic body referred to by Shakhnazarov;

(b) invasion from outer space – an enduring theme of science fiction, recently raised by President Reagan in his correspondence with Gorbachev; or

(c) causes internal to the world civilization – war between components of the civilization, or ecological catastrophe induced by human activity.

Social awareness of the possibility of catastrophe was for a time marginalized by the optimistic outlook on the future promoted by the great philosophies of progress, with their roots in the eighteenth and nineteenth centuries, notably liberalism and Marxism. This progressive outlook, though still dominant, is now somewhat weakened and sobered by growing knowledge of the vulnerability of the environment to human disruption and by fear of the potential destructiveness of modern military technology.

Nevertheless, even in the heyday of optimism some thinkers extrapolated into the future the trend of military technology and predicted that war would at some point become capable of destroying civilization. Even in the eighteenth century Kant forecast that ultimately humanity would find 'eternal peace' either in a treaty banning war or in a 'gigantic cemetery'. Tolstoy and the Russian scientist and philosopher Vernadsky are also among the figures claimed by Soviet writers as prophets of the waiting danger.[10]

Marx, Engels and Lenin, whom Soviet ideologists are obliged to respect as supreme authorities, therefore thought and wrote in a cultural environment which, though dominated by optimistic expectations of social progress, already contained as a minor theme the idea of the possible self-destruction of civilization. And while the inevitability of progress was certainly the preponderant motif in their own thought, they are on record as having uttered occasional comments which indicate that they too were influenced by this minor theme, even if they never publicly elaborated its implications. These comments are now repeatedly recalled by Soviet writers concerned to establish the ideological legitimacy of the catastrophic view of nuclear war.

Thus Engels once remarked that the time would come when the progress of military technology would make war unthinkable.[11] Lenin's widow, Nadezhda Krupskaya, recorded in her memoirs that Lenin had remarked in 1918 that 'a time will come when war will have become so destructive that it will be quite impossible'. In 1920 or 1921 Lenin told his wife of 'a conversation with an engineer who said that an invention is now in store which could destroy a large army at a distance'.[12] That Lenin may have been indirectly aware of the military potential of atomic energy is also suggested by a reminiscence of Armand Hammer, the American businessman who knew Lenin, reported in *Pravda*:

'Lenin looked far ahead,' [said Hammer] ... 'When I was in Moscow [in 1922] I presented to him through one of my colleagues a sculpture purchased in London – a monkey sitting on a little volume of Darwin's *The Origin of Species* examining a human skull. I was told that on receiving the gift Lenin said: "This is what could happen to mankind if it continues to build up weapons of destruction; only monkeys will be left on earth."[13]

There is also a potentially pertinent comment in Marx's *Communist Manifesto*, relating to the history of pre-capitalist civilizations rather than to the development of military technology. Marx's opening description of past history as the history of class struggle allows for not just a progressive, but also an alternative regressive, outcome of class struggle in a given society: 'Freeman and slave, patrician and plebeian, lord and serf, guild-master and journeyman, in a word, oppressor and oppressed ... carried on an uninterrupted ... fight, a fight that each time ended, either in a revolutionary reconstitution of society at large, or in the common ruin of the contending classes.[14]

There is, however, a somewhat later strand of the Marxist tradition which places the danger of destruction of modern civilization squarely at the centre of its outlook. This is the school of thought which holds that capitalism at its 'imperialist' stage is bound to destroy itself by war – and with it the whole of civilization – if allowed to pursue its dynamic of struggle between rival imperialist powers to the end. It is vital that revolutionary action not be indefinitely delayed, and that this fatal process be interrupted by the socialist revolution in good time. The historical alternatives are not 'socialism sooner or later', but 'socialism or barbarism'. This position is associated especially with the name of Rosa Luxemburg, a theorist of revolutionary socialism active mainly in Germany before, during and shortly after the First World War. In Stalin's time, Rosa Luxemburg was a non-person in the Soviet Union and Eastern Europe, but her reputation has since undergone a modest degree of rehabilitation, and she is occasionally quoted as an authority on the war danger. The Central Committee official Vadim Zagladin approvingly quotes the seminal passage which Luxemburg, shocked by the slaughter of the First World War, wrote in 1915:

A single glance around shows us what this return of bourgeois society to barbarism means. This world war is a return to

21

barbarism. The triumph of imperialism leads to a destruction of culture – sporadic during a modern war, and total if the current period of world wars is brought to its logical conclusion. Therefore today we are ... truly facing a choice: either a triumph of imperialism and a collapse of all culture, as in Ancient Rome – extinction, desolation, degeneration and a huge graveyard; or a victory of socialism ...[15]

In fact, the idea of 'socialism or barbarism' recurs frequently in Soviet ideology, even if explicit references to Rosa Luxemburg are usually omitted. Shakhnazarov states quite unequivocally that 'without socialism humanity will perish', on the grounds that the growing gap between developed and underdeveloped countries is bound to generate such tension and conflict as to make an explosion into world war inevitable within 20–50 years.[16] The assumption is made in this type of argument that capitalism is unable, by means of reform, sufficiently to control or moderate such dangerous trends. World socialism therefore becomes necessary not only as a fulfilment of historical law, but as 'the sole road to salvation ... for the whole planet'.[17]

Alternative outlooks on the future

Recognition of the nuclear threat does not lead to any unique outlook on the part of Soviet ideology. On the one hand, realization that the 'class struggle on the international arena' (as Soviet ideology views the East-West conflict) may entail 'the mutual ruin of the contending classes' dictates that the struggle be softened, controlled within safer forms, even if this means postponing its successful culmination. On the other hand, if it is believed that without the victory of world socialism (or at least substantial progress towards it) humanity will perish within the next few decades, then this might be expected to impart a sense of urgency to the struggle, which may come into conflict with the requirements of caution. The political implications of the nuclear threat therefore depend crucially on the answer to the question: Is a stable and secure peace possible in a world shared with capitalism? If such a peace is possible, it may prove a satisfactory medium-term alternative to catastrophe. If not, then completion of the transition to a 'socialist' world can be the only escape from the trap.

4
PEACE AND THE CORRELATION OF FORCES

The view of East-West detente as a natural outcome of the growth in Soviet power has its origins in Soviet ideology of the Khrushchev period, but it was in the mid-1970s, when detente at last seemed secured, that it acquired its most complete form as the dominant tendency in the foreign-policy analysis of Party ideologists. This view, outlined in the present chapter, will serve as our starting-point when, in the next chapter, we embark on our exploration of more recent Soviet perspectives.

'Peaceful coexistence': struggle plus cooperation

It has been pointed out many times that 'peaceful coexistence' is not a synonym of harmony, but is conceived of in Soviet ideology as a form of unceasing struggle between East and West, constrained by the need to avoid open war. This does not mean, however, as some argue, that the Soviet Union defines peaceful coexistence as 'a cold coexistence without war', carrying 'no connotations of goodwill or cooperation whatsoever'.[1] That a measure of cooperation has its place in East-West relations is implicit in Soviet approval and support of many UN and other international activities,[2] and recognition of shared interests in various fields (e.g. nuclear non-proliferation). Since 1976, when Brezhnev declared in his Report to the 25th Party Congress that global problems require the cooperation of all countries,[3] the formal status of the cooperative aspect has been steadily raised.

Thus cooperation is recognized, and at the same time continuing struggle is by no means denied. The result is a unity of opposites: 'Peaceful coexistence has a double nature. It is a system of cooperation, and a special form of class struggle, between States with different social systems.'[4]

The military philosophers Milovidov and Zhdanov break down the concept of peaceful coexistence into seven components: four kinds of cooperation (political, economic, scientific-technical and cultural) and three kinds of struggle (political struggle, economic rivalry and ideological conflict).[5]

Within the limits of the 'unity of cooperation and struggle' (or vice versa) there is scope for differences in emphasis. Some writers put more stress on cooperation, others on struggle, but none goes so far as to repudiate either aspect of the relationship. The stance of a writer is perhaps most sharply signalled by the words chosen to refer to the other participant in the interaction – from 'enemy' through 'adversary/opponent' and 'rival/competitor' to 'partner', not forgetting the non-committal expression 'the other side'.

Socialism = peace; capitalism = war

In the simplest version of the ideology, there is a straightforward identification of 'socialism' with 'peace', and of 'capitalism' with the danger of war. For socialism contains no social forces with a stake in war, so that its world victory will be 'the full and final guarantee of peace among peoples'. Capitalism, by contrast, has an inherent tendency to give rise to war, both wars between capitalist powers ('inter-imperialist war') and war against socialism. It follows that the interests of peace and the interests of socialism must be the same. Thus, although in the short term the 'struggle for peace' and the 'struggle for socialism' are to a greater or lesser degree distinct (a matter of legitimate argument), if the long view is taken there is a single 'struggle for peace and socialism' (or 'struggle for peace and social progress').

The long-term historical trend of the current era is the cumulative change of the correlation of forces – that is, the ratio of political, military and economic power between the socialist and capitalist blocs – to the advantage of socialism. The orthodoxy of the 1970s held that this advance of socialism in the world is accompanied by a progressive strengthening of peace and diminution of the war danger. First of all, the social basis of war is abolished in more and more countries, which add their weight to the influence of the peace policy of the socialist community. Secondly, the capitalist States which remain are increasingly effectively deterred from aggression as the relative military strength of the 'forces of peace' grows, and are obliged to adapt themselves to the new world realities.

If the advance of socialism strengthens peace, the strengthening of peace in turn facilitates the advance of socialism. 'Detente creates the purest conditions, those most free of artificial obstacles, for the development of social processes.' Detente enables the socialist countries to reduce their military burden, and (some add) to develop democracy more easily and overcome 'deformations' caused by international tension. Anti-communism becomes a less effective ideological weapon against working-class struggle in the capitalist countries. Detente in general eases imperialist pressure on the revolutionary movement, reducing the danger of 'export of counter-revolution'.[6] 'Recent decades prove that the revolutionary forces have achieved their greatest results . . . under conditions of detente.'[7] Thus the 1970s saw the victory of the national-liberation movement in Indochina, Angola, Mozambique, Ethiopia and other countries, the fall of fascist regimes in Greece, Portugal and Spain, the breaking of the blockade of Cuba and the international recognition of East Germany.[8] This does not mean that detente benefits *only* socialism: it is an objective necessity for the survival of all humanity, and socialism advances under conditions of confrontation as well, although more slowly.

It is an implication of the model that socialism will in time acquire military as well as other kinds of superiority over capitalism. This is sometimes, though rarely, spelled out. 'Whatever superiority the forces of the new rising world may in future acquire over those of the old departing world,' Shakhnazarov assures us, 'it is alien to the nature of socialism to put its stake on victory in war.'[9] But is there a logical contradiction between this perspective and the statements of Soviet leaders and commentators since 1977 recognizing military equilibrium as 'objectively a safeguard of world peace' and repudiating the goal of military superiority?[10]

It may be that the two types of statement simply refer to different time-scales. That is, superiority may still be regarded as desirable in the very long term, but in the short-to-medium term parity is the only realistic – and of course the preferable – alternative to Western superiority. The nuclear/conventional distinction may well also be pertinent. The repudiation of superiority at the nuclear level is linked to doubt concerning the possibility of victory in nuclear war. But it is hard to see how, short of total disarmament, the transition to worldwide socialism could occur without the socialist side gaining superiority in conventional forces in the final stages.

Permutations

Various complications may motivate permutations of this simple model:

(1)   The experience of war between socialist countries casts doubt on whether the world victory of socialism is *sufficient* to eliminate the war danger. Those ideologists who face up to this issue attribute inter-socialist war to 'the immaturity of socialist social relations and consciousness'. It is admitted that peace will be fully secure only when socialism has become worldwide and, in addition, has attained 'a sufficiently high level of maturity in all spheres of social life'.[11]

(2)   On the other hand, the phenomenon of war might be 'excluded from the life of society with capitalism still remaining in part of the world'[12] – that is, the world victory of socialism may not be *necessary* to eliminate the war danger. This hypothesis, however, is denied by harder-line ideologists, who argue that, however secure detente may seem, 'the existence of imperialism [i.e. capitalism], the presence of an objective basis alien to peace, preserves the possibility of a return to tension and even to war.'[13] The key issue is the closeness of the connection between capitalism and militarism.

(3)   There may be deviation in the opposite direction from the historical path of the proportionate advance of peace and of socialism. Instead of sensibly adapting themselves to the coming world victory of socialism, the remaining capitalist States may react in a suicidally irrational manner.

(4)   Even if the long-term identity between the interests of peace and of socialism is granted, this does not prevent short-term collisions of interest from occurring, since Soviet support of revolutionary forces may entail occasional confrontations fraught with the risk of nuclear war.

(5)   The long-term tendency for the correlation of forces to change to the advantage of socialism does not rule out temporary reverse movements to the disadvantage of socialism.[14]

(6)   Although detente was always in the 1970s attributed primarily to the strengthening of the position of world socialism, some accounts did allot a subsidiary role to the factor of economic and technological interdependence. 'Economic needs . . . compel us [on both sides] to search for ways of cooperating in the fields of science and technology and of developing . . . trade relations.'[15] This motive received less stress in the later than in the early 1970s, when Brezhnev was pressing for very large-scale trade between the USSR and the West, a development prevented by internal political resistance as well as by external obstacles.[16]

Stages on the road to peace and socialism

Although Party ideology, as it had taken shape by the 1970s, conceived of the transition of the world from capitalism to socialism, and thereby from open or latent war to secure peace, as a continuous process, it also distinguished a series of qualitatively different stages of the era of transition, each lasting a number of decades. A definite level of war danger corresponds to each stage. While the conditions for further progress mature during any given stage, the most important changes in the world situation tend to be concentrated in the relatively short periods of movement from one stage to the next. The number of stages is six, or perhaps seven:

(1)   In the decades leading up to 1917, capitalism, though under challenge from the working-class movement, dominated the whole world. In this period the capitalist system, as Lenin argued, attained its highest stage, imperialism, which has an inherent drive towards inter-imperialist war.

(2)   The Russian Revolution created the first socialist country. However, in the period between the two world wars the influence of socialism over events was still too weak to avert war, which Soviet doctrine at that time correctly regarded as inevitable.

(3)   The isolation of the USSR as the sole socialist country was overcome in the aftermath of the Second World War, which saw the emergence of the socialist bloc. 'The change in the correlation of forces after World War II opened up real perspectives of preventing

war.'[17] After some delay the new situation gained proper official recognition from 1956 in Khrushchev's doctrine of peaceful coexistence. (That is, after 1945 Stalin's doctrine of the inevitability of war had become incorrect.)

(4) The strengthening of the position of socialism brought about by the USSR achieving rough strategic parity with the USA in the late 1960s made it possible to move at the beginning of the 1970s to the next stage, that of detente. Detente 'bears witness to the fact that the ruling circles of the capitalist countries have begun to recognize the impossibility of deciding the outcome of the struggle to their advantage by military means'.[18] Detente marks a significant improvement in international security, but a substantial threat of war remains. In particular, the danger presented by local wars cannot yet be eliminated:

> Within the existing correlation of forces ... there is not yet the possibility of fully excluding aggression and the local wars associated with it, but there is already the possibility of sharply limiting the sphere of arbitrary action of imperialist reaction.[19]

Nevertheless, detente, which was expected to persist, would permit the gradual diminution of the war danger through the final decades of the twentieth century and the opening decades of the twenty-first.

(5) The next stage is to be reached when socialism clearly gains the position of the predominant system in the world, even though capitalism remains in a number of important countries. By this time, a majority of countries will have at least 'taken the path of socialism', though many of them may still be in a transitional state. Above all, this stage is marked by the turn away from capitalism of some more of the economically most developed countries, the crucial region in this respect being Western Europe.

The new stage is expected to entail greatly enhanced prospects for world peace and disarmament, though, as we have noted, there is disagreement about whether complete disarmament can be achieved and war fully excluded from the life of society while capitalism still exists.

(6) Eventually the remaining capitalist countries also make the transition to socialism, so that socialism has won out on a world scale. Whether this means that world peace is permanently guaranteed depends on whether or not it is assumed that the problem of

tensions between socialist States has by this point been fully resolved. If it is assumed, as Shakhnazarov does, that the problem is likely to persist into the period of worldwide socialism, then this period has to be broken down into two stages – before and after socialist international relations take on their mature form – and peace is completely secure only in the last stage.

There is indication that some Soviet ideologists have envisaged a very rough timetable for the coming of the next two stages (5 and 6). Shakhnazarov tabulates forecasts of developments which he regards as more or less probable within a time-span of fifty years – that is, by about 2030. He considers it 'very probable' that there will have been 'a significant expansion of the world system of socialism', though he admits as low-probability variants 'the full victory of socialism in the world' at one extreme and 'the restoration of capitalism in particular [socialist] countries' at the other. His 'probable' forecasts provide for 'the transition to the path of socialism of the majority of countries of the world, including some of the economically most developed countries', together with 'an increase in the number of countries of the transitional type'.[20] In other words, movement to the next stage is thought likely by 2030.

Another suggestion of timing is provided by Kosolapov, the former editor of *Kommunist*, who looks forward to worldwide 'revolutionary renewal' within 50–100 years – that is, by 2030–2080.[21] This also is consistent with the claim made by the defector Arkady Shevchenko to the effect that 'Moscow believes that eventually it will be supreme – not necessarily in this century but certainly in the next – in the competition between the socialist and capitalist systems.'[22]

5

THE ORTHODOXY
IN CRISIS

The ideological crisis arises
The orthodoxy of the 1970s was built on the conviction that history guarantees irreversible progress towards a more secure peace. The turn to detente had been the product of 'new realities', of the shift in the global correlation of forces in general and of the attainment of strategic parity by the USSR in particular. Indeed, it was 'the surest criterion of the current correlation of forces'.[1] Within this framework the return to East-West confrontation at the turn of the 1980s appeared deeply anomalous, frontally challenging the ability of established doctrine to explain events. It became necessary to assert that American ruling circles have a grossly deficient perception of reality. The foreign affairs analyst Alexei Arbatov posed the puzzle as follows:

Return to [the Cold War], it would have seemed, had been securely barred by the events of the 1960s and 1970s – the failure of US aggression in Vietnam, the radical change in the global correlation of forces ... It was as if all this did not exist for the new American leadership, as if they had knocked a 'window' through history and missed these events ...

If the positive changes in American policy [in the 1970s] were conditioned by objective circumstances ..., then what has become of these circumstances [now]? Why does the Reagan administration find it possible not to take account of them, and in general to deny their existence? ... [So] which was a passing chance development, and which was objectively inevitable and long-term in American policy: the transition to detente ... or the return to confrontation?[2]

The strength of the 1970s orthodoxy may account in part for the slowness with which Soviet analysts of American politics came to appreciate the seriousness and durability of the new hard line of the Reagan administration. Writing in 1980, just after Reagan's election, the Americanologist Trofimenko could see no difference between the two presidential candidates, and hoped for 'a constructive approach to American-Soviet relations' from the new administration.[3] 'The new masters of the White House', predicted his colleague Pechatnov, 'will undoubtedly discover that in practice they have to measure up not to their pre-election rhetoric but to the objective realities of the contemporary world.'[4] A year later Zhurkin, a deputy director of the USA Institute, found the confrontational strategy of the Reagan administration 'increasingly clear', but nevertheless predicted that it 'will have to face up to the realities ..., whether it wishes to do so or not'.[5]

But time passed, and the imperialist ruling circles showed little sign of 'facing up to the realities'. Instead, it was Soviet commentators who found themselves faced with the reality that their own ideology was now in a state of crisis.

Types of response to the ideological crisis

It is useful to distinguish four types of perspective on the future formulated by Soviet ideologists in response to the crisis of the 1970s orthodoxy:

(1) Some maintain the expectation that the simultaneous advance towards peace and socialism will after a certain period be resumed. These analysts do not agree among themselves on such matters as the reasons for the present interruption of the advance and its likely duration, but they share the inclination to preserve the orthodoxy of the 1970s, adapted as seems necessary to account for a temporary return to Cold War.

(2)   Other ideologists, stressing the strength of the factors working both for and against detente, predict over the foreseeable future fluctuations in the international climate, which will take the form either of relatively predictable cycles or of unpredictable zig-zags.

(3)   Yet others break radically with the optimistic perspective of the 1970s and revert to the earlier Bolshevik view that as socialism strengthens its position in the world the hostility between the two systems tends to increase. This view occurs in moderate and in extreme versions, occasionally going so far as to imply that war may once again become inevitable.

(4)   Finally, there are those who abandon the 1970s orthodoxy, but re-establish an optimistic outlook on a different basis. The advance towards peace is freed of its dependence on a simultaneous advance towards socialism. Instead, it is argued that the material foundation for cooperation and detente now lies in the increasing interdependence of the two systems in their economic development, in their security requirements and in their need to tackle jointly the global problems faced by humanity as a whole. The advance towards socialism is not repudiated, but it is deferred to a later time when peace will be secure, its immediate priority being downgraded.

For the sake of convenience we might refer to these types of perspective as 'interruption perspectives', 'fluctuation perspectives', 'confrontation perspectives' and 'interdependence perspectives'.

(a)   Interruption perspectives

In the simplest of the interruption perspectives, the normal course of history is held to have been diverted for a time purely as a result of the accidental psychological characteristics of the members of the Reagan administration. There is therefore no need to search for 'deep' historical explanations. President Reagan and his colleagues are inclined to take an absolutist approach to politics because they are novices deficient in foreign-policy experience and in general culture.[6] The director of the USA Institute, G. Arbatov, a prominent advocate of this interpretation in the early Reagan years, expressed in 1982 the hope that 'the continuing policy process [would] strengthen realistic principles' within the administration, and reassured himself with the thought that after Reagan there would be a new and more reasonable US president with whom the USSR could do business.[7]

One means of easing, if not eliminating, the problem of accounting for the contrast between the detente of the 1970s and the confrontation of the 1980s is the retrospective devaluation of the progress made in the 1970s. Soviet analysts, like Western ones, have concluded that detente was not as firmly established as it appeared to be at the time. As in the West, some analysts argue, as Yakovlev does, that the other side was never seriously committed to detente: 'Detente was a tactical expedient for the US; the ruling circles did not regard it as a long-term policy.'[8] Others make less sweeping re-evaluations that enable detente still to be viewed as a big step forward. 'Events of the past few years have demonstrated how strong the enemies of detente remain.'[9]

Downgrading the detente of the 1970s displaces rather than solves the ideological problem, for it merely shifts the question why strategic parity fails to produce the results expected of it to an earlier time-frame. Those who try to preserve the long-term integrity of the old orthodoxy without explaining Reaganism away as a meaningless aberration are driven to argue that 'the adaptation of the US ruling class to the new world situation' is indeed proceeding, but 'in a painful and contradictory way'.[10] But the growing pains will, after an interval of uncertain duration, be overcome.

As an example of an interpretation on these lines, we may take that of Alexander Yakovlev at the time when he was director of the Institute of World Economy and International Relations (he is now a Central Committee Secretary and a close adviser to Gorbachev). Yakovlev accuses of 'complacency' those (like G. Arbatov) who regard the turn of the USA from detente 'as a chance moment in history, a moment of an irrational nature, and attribute it to the personal qualities of President Reagan'. For Yakovlev, the new offensive strategy of imperialism is a purposeful attempt to recover lost economic, political and military-strategic positions:

There is a certain objective basis for the socio-political anxiety ... increasingly felt by Washington's ruling circles over the past 10–15 years ... The quickening pace of historical progress step by step narrows the potential and space for manoeuvre of imperialism.[11]

However, the current militaristic reaction of imperialism to its decline will not succeed in its aims, for 'adaptation to the real world development is inevitable, ... a historical imperative for capitalist society ... Sooner or later a new detente will replace confrontation with the regularity of a historical tendency smoothing over an arbitrary zigzag.' But this, he says, can happen 'only if the forces of socialism ... continue resolutely to counteract the capitalist system, which still has considerable reserves for economic and political manoeuvre and development.'[12]

The attainment of a reliable detente remains, then, a function of the correlation of forces, but the correlation reached in the 1970s, contrary to what then appeared to be the case, was inadequate. The conclusion is spelled out even more clearly, in 1984 and again in 1987, by the deputy head of the Central Committee International Department, V. V. Zagladin: what is needed to strengthen peace is 'an increase in the economic, political and military might of world socialism'.[13] In this perspective, it is the premature detente of the 1970s, not the current confrontation, which is really the anomaly.

(b)   Fluctuation perspectives

Interruption perspectives allow for fluctuations in the international situation during some period of 'adaptation', but retain confidence that this phase will be passed through in the not too distant future. However, once it is granted that 'objective' changes in the correlation of forces do not automatically bring about corresponding 'subjective' changes in the consciousness of the Western ruling class, the analyst easily comes to feel uncertain about how, when and even whether the fluctuations in Western policy can be brought to an end:

> The American power elite has never been enchanted by detente, [which is] not [its] most habitual attitude ... Objective realities can sometimes ... compel people ... to change their attitudes. But this does not mean that such changes come easily or that they are irreversible. The old, the habitual ... tends to come back to the fore at the slightest provocation.[14]

If 'habitual attitudes' and 'objective realities' are regarded as influences of comparable power, then the inference drawn by the publicist Alexander Bovin seems plausible – that is, that there is 'a cyclical character to the evolution of Soviet-American relations, an alternation between periods of detente and confrontation', reflecting the confrontation between different groups within the US ruling class.[15] If, as has been hypothesized,[16] each phase of the cycle lasts about ten years, a period of detente can be expected in the 1990s and renewed confrontation at the beginning of the next century.

A more subtle fluctuation perspective was suggested by Yuri Krasin, Pro-Rector of the Central Committee Academy of Social Sciences, in 1981:

> Steps ... towards the restructuring of international relations are not ... simply the result of the growing strength of socialism. The world system has an inner logic which is determined by the complex interplay of all of its constituent elements ... Periods of relaxation of tension ... alternate with outbursts of war hysteria ...

Krasin proceeds to observe that the achievement of detente is greatly dependent also on the political initiative and good judgment of the ruling parties of the socialist countries – an unusual hint that responsibility for East-West tension may not lie solely with the Western side.[17]

(c) Confrontation perspectives

The ideologists attached to the first two types of perspective see the setback to detente as a fluctuation – either a single isolated fluctuation or the first in a series. In confrontation perspectives this is rejected as an 'illusion'. At the minimum it is argued, as in a leading article in *Kommunist* in early 1984, that the dangerous international situation is determined by factors which 'have deep socio-economic roots' and so 'may be of a long-term nature'.[18] But the argument may go further, to deny the long-term tendency for detente to accompany the advance of socialism and to assert instead an opposite tendency – that is, that as the process of social transformation advances the capitalist class becomes increasingly aggressive and 'the opposition of the old and the new systems more and more clearly takes on the form of a general split'.[19] Reference may here be made to a statement by Lenin dating from the civil war years: 'The power of revolution ... strengthens the power of resistance of the bourgeoisie. The more we are victorious, the more will the capitalist exploiters learn to unite and go over to more decisive attacks.'[20]

A notable literary exponent of the confrontation perspective is Alexander Prokhanov, a writer who has in recent years devoted himself to contemporary military themes. In 1985 Prokhanov called upon his fellow writers to realize that the easy days of detente are over and that an era of confrontation is commencing, so they should stop writing about dreamy characters who commune with nature and start portraying more heroic types.[21] In February 1987 he greeted the first Soviet nuclear-test explosion after the moratorium as the only language the American militarists understand, ridiculing the idea that it serves any purpose 'to send them our schoolgirl as a messenger of peace'. 'Again history, held still for a moment, moved along its gloomy path.'[22]

Most of those who expect prolonged confrontation think nuclear war a possible outcome of it, but do not expect the West deliberately to seek nuclear war. Yet there are others, such as the former editor of *Kommunist*, Richard Kosolapov, who do not rule out the possibility that 'nuclear maniacs' might choose nuclear war, even in full awareness of its consequences, rather than gracefully accept their own demise:

> Swallowed up in the abyss of its general crisis, capitalism becomes especially dangerous. In ancient times, slave-holders and feudal lords ordered that their wives, servants and slaves be buried with them when they died. In our times, capitalism, in leaving the historical scene, is ready to take with it all life on earth.[23]

The writer Alexander Krivitsky argues that any ruling class facing defeat will blow up the world if it can. Would the European aristocrats not have used nuclear weapons to prevent the French Revolution? Would Hitler from his Berlin bunker not have 'blotted out the light with malicious joy'? The modern capitalist class can hardly be expected to act differently, and it is 'an enormous misfortune' that nuclear weapons have fallen into its hands.[24]

No Soviet writer openly states that war is inevitable, and negative trends do not exclude the possibility that the forces of peace may manage to avert war until the safety of world socialism is reached. Nevertheless the view that nuclear holocaust is the most likely end-point of social development does seem implicit in ideas of this kind. That such despairing outlooks became widespread among the Soviet public in the early 1980s is suggested by a report by the political commentator of *The Literary Gazette*, Fedor Burlatsky, of letters received from the magazine's readers about war and peace. 'Some readers doubt the possibility of implementing in practice the principles of peaceful coexistence in the new international conditions'; others conclude that a third world war is inevitable. Burlatsky advises readers not 'boundlessly to dramatize the situation'.[25]

Pessimism of a more restrained kind is characteristic of military writers. Even in the 1970s these did not rate highly the potential of detente. They state that imperialism tends to become more aggressive as socialism advances, but also that the tendency can be controlled and war averted (though war is always possible). The military perspective is a relatively unchanging one, minimizing the significance of fluctuations between relative detente and confrontation. Thus Gen.-Col. Gareyev, Deputy Chief of the General Staff, ridicules unidentified 'bourgeois' – but probably, by implication, Soviet – ideologists for overreacting first in one direction and then in the other:

> In the 1970s, when there appeared a tendency towards the relaxation of international tension, some bourgeois ideologists were writing about change in the aggressive essence of imperialism, about its love for peace. Now, when the world situation has become sharper, they are on the contrary crying about the inevitability of war.[26]

In Gareyev's view, 'at the contemporary stage and in the foreseeable future, the threat can be slowed down or postponed, but the threat cannot be completely eliminated.'[27]

(d) Interdependence perspectives

In the perspectives examined so far, a secure peace either is not attainable at all in the near future or is conditional on the further advance of socialism in the world. Recent years have seen the emergence of an alternative optimistic perspective which views detente as a natural product of long-term tendencies towards growing interdependence on a global level.

It is held, first of all, that peace is needed so urgently that it cannot wait on long-term transformations of the socio-economic make-up of the world. 'The problem of the eradication of war', writes

Grigoryan, 'must be basically solved during the life of the present generation.'[28] Far from peace depending on the prior advance of socialism, 'elimination of the danger of nuclear war is a prerequisite of further successes of socialism and communism, of social progress as a whole.'[29]

The strategy of 'peace first, socialism later' was advocated in 1986 by Yuri Krasin. Since 'the very preconditions of social progress' are dependent on peace, 'the struggle for peace becomes for communists an independent strategic goal, which has undoubted priority relative to other goals ... The struggle for peace does not in itself lead to fundamental transformations of the capitalist system, and does not pursue such goals ... The success of the struggle for peace does not resolve the question "who-whom" on the international arena.'[30] (The reference is to Lenin's formula for which side will win out over the other.) The struggle between capitalism and socialism is to be carried through to its final outcome in a secure demilitarized environment.

The relationship between the time perspectives of the struggle for peace and the struggle for socialism is also the point at issue in a dispute over Burlatsky's concept of 'the planning of peace', by which he means an agreed programme of joint East-West measures aimed at the prevention of nuclear war.[31] Shakhnazarov criticizes this concept as inaccurate, preferring that of 'organized peace'.[32] A reviewer of Shakhnazarov's book offers the following clarification of the matter:

> I think ... that this counterposition [of 'planned peace' to 'organized peace'] is based on a misunderstanding. When one speaks of the planning of world peace, one has in mind, first, the relatively foreseeable future and, second, not the whole of social development but the evolution of the system of international relations ... As for 'organized peace', ... here one has in mind the distant future, when a radical change will occur in the conditions of the whole of social development on earth.[33]

Yet this distinction, which sets elimination of the war danger as the overriding immediate task and relegates radical social change to the distant future, can hardly be acceptable to those for whom the struggles for peace and for socialism are interdependent and to be pursued jointly.

The strategy of 'peace first, socialism later', however, faces two ideological obstacles, which we shall discuss in Chapters 7 and 8 respectively. First, it must be shown that, notwithstanding the Leninist thesis of the inherently militaristic nature of imperialism, a secure peace between socialism and capitalism is possible. Second, a new factor must be cited as the material basis of peace, supplementing or replacing the factor of further improvement in the correlation of forces.

This factor is growing global interdependence in its various forms. States can no longer provide for their security in the nuclear age by means of unilateral military preparations: the only reliable security is common security, arrived at by political methods. Other global problems too, such as preservation of the environment and the provision of energy and raw materials, can be solved only by international cooperation. Finally, integration of the world economy multiplies the ties of interdependence linking together the economic development of socialist, capitalist and underdeveloped countries.

Like all abstract schemes, this classification of perspectives is simpler and more clear-cut than the material it is designed to organize. For example, we have focused on the views of Soviet ideologists concerning the relations between the USSR and the capitalist world taken as a whole, even though a man such as Yakovlev combines an optimistic outlook on relations with some parts of the capitalist world (Western Europe, Japan) with a deeply pessimistic outlook on relations with another part (the USA). Nevertheless, some may find the scheme helpful as a starting-point.

6
THE VALUE OF PEACE

It is not only in the context of long-term changes in the world situation that the relationship between the goals of peace and of communism presents a problem. The makers of foreign policy are quite frequently forced to make immediate choices between accepting what they regard as setbacks to communist interests and undertaking actions fraught with some degree of risk to world peace. First we briefly consider expressed Soviet attitudes to risk-taking in the post-Stalin period before Gorbachev. We then analyse signs of shifting attitudes under Gorbachev as reflected in the revision of the theory of revolutionary struggle and in the reassessment of the status of 'peace' as a value.

The Soviet attitude to risk-taking before Gorbachev

Soviet leaders have always been loath to run the risk of war with a powerful adversary, and 'adventurism' has always been repudiated as an error by Soviet ideology.[1] However, *some* level of risk has been judged acceptable when interests of sufficient importance have been at stake. Thus Khrushchev in his memoirs confesses himself afraid of war, but immediately adds: 'That doesn't mean I think we should pay any price to avoid war. Certainly we shouldn't back down at the expense of our self-respect, our authority and our prestige in the world.'[2] And Brezhnev told the kidnapped Czech leadership in 1968 that he would still have invaded Czechoslovakia, even at the cost of risking a new war.[3]

In arguments defending risky Soviet actions against criticism from within the international communist movement, Party officials have pointed to the losses to communist positions in the world that Soviet inaction would have entailed: 'The "critics" do not think of what could have happened in Cuba in 1962, in Hungary in 1956, in Czechoslovakia in 1968 and in Afghanistan after the victory of the April 1978 revolution, if imperialism had been given a free hand.'[4] The implication is that peace does not automatically outweigh other values, that there are definite limits on the price which it is acceptable to pay for it. This is indeed spelled out in the tough editorial published in the January 1984 issue of the journal of the Institute of Philosophy: '[We] will go far for the sake of peace ... But if the Soviet side is ready to go far, that does not mean it will go to any lengths whatsoever. We shall protect our ideas and values, ... our right to independent development, with all the means necessary.'[5]

The most substantial discussions of risk-taking in Soviet literature are those of Georgy Shakhnazarov, who as a senior official in one of the foreign-policy departments of the Central Committee must have personal policy-making experience. Recognizing that prevention of nuclear war is a priority task, he nevertheless justifies a certain level of risk-taking as being in the longer-term interests of peace itself.[6]

Soviet foreign policy, he explains, is not 'de-ideologized great-power politics'. Political and military action taken by the USSR in solidarity with revolutionary movements has periodically brought it into direct or indirect confrontation with the USA, so that only the diplomatic efforts of both sides have averted nuclear war. 'If ... the USSR were guided by egoistically conceived considerations of advantage, then it would simply avoid the risk of confrontation.'

However, progress towards world socialism is essential if humanity is 'to escape from the dangers of the nuclear age', for capitalism is 'unable to lead humanity away from the abyss'.[7] Therefore the long-term interests of peace and of socialism are identical. The 'objective contradictions' that exist are not between the interests of peace and of socialism, but between the current and the long-term interests of both. These have to be judiciously balanced, for 'if we were to work only for tomorrow, or only for today, we would have no future.' A certain level of risk for the sake of progress is acceptable.

The Soviet foreign-policy maker, Shakhnazarov muses, faces difficult choices. No general formula can 'solve the very complex, at times head-breaking, tasks that arise in practice'. It is likely that on certain occasions excessive risks were taken because 'the sharpness of the international situation was not adequately taken into account'. On the other hand, future interests may be unduly subordinated to current ones. Whether this occurs 'greatly depends on the will, the theoretical training and the moral qualities of political leaders'. An extended metaphor drives the point home:

> Imagine a man who has fallen into a quagmire. On the one hand, any sharp movement may prove fatal to him. On the other hand, he is in danger of perishing, and not with great delay, if he does not try to pull himself on to firm land. He has no choice but to move forward while maintaining the utmost caution.

This perception of the situation lends a note of urgency to the deliberations of those who share it about communist prospects. For example, Shakhnazarov remarks that failure to achieve an effective left-wing coalition of communists and social-democrats in the countries of Western Europe 'will mean ... the loss or half-loss of 15–20 more years, time precious ... for all humanity'.[8] Only 'the revolutionary renewal of the social face of the world', argues Kosolapov, can avert catastrophe, and 'the last quarter of the twentieth century is to a large degree decisive'.[9]

The risk of nuclear war depends on whether revolutionary movements adopt armed or peaceful methods of struggle, and on the likelihood that local conflicts which draw in the superpowers will escalate to world war. In the 1970s, such events as the failure of the peaceful path in Chile and the success of armed struggle in Nicaragua led Soviet foreign affairs analysts to lay increasing stress on the need for armed struggle.[10] Soviet writers have always held that the escalation of local conflicts is possible but not inevitable. However, whereas in the period 1956–68 their main emphasis was on the danger of escalation, the main emphasis in the period 1969–81 was on the feasibility of deterring escalation.[11]

The revision of revolutionary theory
An early indication of a heightened Soviet aversion to risk-taking under Gorbachev appears at the beginning of 1986 in Krasin's exposition of the new peace strategy, discussed in the last chapter.

Refuting the view that a stable and guaranteed peace is attainable only with the abolition of capitalism, Krasin warns that 'this position holds within itself the danger of adventurism, because it latently encourages the "pushing" of the revolutionary process, allegedly for the sake of achieving peace'.[12] By implication, the previously dominant perception of the urgency of socialist advance for the cause of peace is blamed for the taking of unjustified risks in foreign policy. Once struggle for peace is disentangled from the struggle for socialism, the slow maturation of revolutionary conditions can be accepted with greater equanimity.

The question of revising revolutionary strategy was taken up by Anatoly Dobrynin soon after his appointment by Gorbachev in March 1986 as Central Committee Secretary in charge of the International Department. Speaking before a conference of Soviet natural and social scientists, Dobrynin called for 'the development and deepening of Marxist-Leninist theory of the world revolutionary process . . . under the conditions of the nuclear age', in order to ensure that the contest between the two systems take exclusively peaceful forms.[13]

We might regard as a response to this call an article on revolutionary prospects contributed to the *Pravda* column 'Questions of theory' in November 1986 by the historian and theorist of revolution Ye. Plimak. Marxists have in the past looked upon violence as the midwife of history, but 'in the nuclear age, . . . violence can readily turn from the midwife of history into its gravedigger'. The 'need for profound changes in political thinking . . . to find a way out of the critical situation' applies to Marxist as well as to bourgeois theory. Since 'all local conflicts . . . have a tendency to grow into regional, and even world, conflicts, . . . the nuclear age requires that revolutionary forces be extremely circumspect in deciding upon armed struggle'. Although dictatorial regimes or military intervention by imperialist powers ('export of counter-revolution') may even now make armed struggle unavoidable, in all other circumstances peaceful compromise forms of struggle must be developed and used, even if this entails 'a more prolonged and gradual process of transformation, with possible retreats'.[14]

There appears to be some opposition from military ideologists to such a selective withdrawal of Soviet approval for armed struggle. Thus Gen.-Lieut. Professor Serebryannikov follows up a justification of Soviet military action in Afghanistan by attacking 'harmful pacifist theories current in the West', according to which armed national-liberation struggle is outdated in the nuclear age because its political consequences may endanger peace.[15] Published in February 1987, this is much more plausibly interpreted as a riposte to Plimak than as a real criticism of Western pacifism. The deduction should not be made that the Soviet military are prepared to accept a high risk of war. On the contrary, military writers also stress the need for 'restrained and circumspect behaviour' on the part of all States.[16] Their main point of difference with civilian analysts seems to be a much less alarmist assessment of the likelihood of escalation from local conflict to nuclear war.

Reassessment of the status of 'peace' as a value

In 1971 UNESCO published a paper on 'the planning of world peace' by the Soviet political scientist and publicist Fedor Burlatsky. One of the main reasons why the paper could not be published in the USSR itself during the Brezhnev period was that in it Burlatsky defines world peace as 'an all-human heritage, *an absolute value*, in contradistinction to relative values which are of significance to particular States, nations and social groups' (italics in original). As examples of such relative values, he mentions national greatness and State prestige. The preservation of peace must be regarded as 'the supreme value and supreme task of world policy'. Burlatsky complains that 'not only in the practical activity of States but also in academic investigations, intermediate goals often overshadow the basic goal and main value of world policy.'[17]

What is ideologically controversial here is the recognition of an absolute value, for Marxism-Leninism has traditionally insisted on the relative nature of all social or moral values. It should be noted that defining 'peace' as the supreme or highest value in a hierarchy of values is not controversial in this sense. A supreme value can still be commensurable with lesser values and therefore relative. An absolute value is incommensurable with relative values: it is impossible to justify ever putting it at any risk.

In his presentation of the 1970s orthodoxy, Shakhnazarov is determined to deny peace such an exalted status: 'The problem of peace can be regarded . . . from different points of view. The solution will be one thing if at the centre of view is set simply the requirement that humanity survive, and quite another if one considers survival insufficient and takes into account requirements of a higher social nature.'[18] While Shakhnazarov's ideal leader is a careful strategist, weighing gains to socialism against possible risks to peace, Burlatsky's is the responsible statesman, a rather de-ideologized figure who is concerned first and foremost with consolidating peace and 'leaves questions relating to the nature of social systems to scholars'.[19]

In the post-Brezhnev period the concept of 'absolute values' has ceased to be taboo. Burlatsky has had his statements concerning peace as an absolute value published several times in the USSR since 1982.[20] Yu. A. Zhdanov, the Rector of Rostov University, has written similarly in *Pravda* about 'the absolute value of human life, before which any partial, local, group, national or regional interests are obliged to give way'.[21]

The elevation of 'peace' above 'socialism' as an absolute value has not, however, gone unopposed. Academician Fedoseyev, long a leading ideologist, has adopted the evasive stance that communists do not counterpose the interests of social progress to the interests of preservation of human life: these are jointly supreme.[22] V.V. Denisov, a sector head at the Institute of Philosophy, condemns '"supra-Party" and "supra-class" positions on questions of peace ... and other all-human values' as utopian, reaffirming that 'Marxism shows the relative, historically transient nature of all ethical principles and moral categories, the incorrectness of their metaphysical absolutization.'[23]

The controversy has been echoed in a muted form at the very top. Speaking with writers from various countries in October 1986, Gorbachev said:

Lenin in his time expressed an idea of colossal depth – concerning the priority of the interests of social development, of all-human values, over the interests of one or another class. Today, in the nuclear age, the importance of this idea is felt especially sharply. And I would very much wish that in the other part of the world also they should understand and accept the thesis of the priority of the all-human value of peace over all others to which different people are attached.[24]

Although Gorbachev stops short of using the word 'absolute' here, the formulation is very close to that pioneered by Burlatsky. It is clearly implied that conflicts of interest may exist between peace and socialism, as between peace and capitalism, and that in both cases peace must always come first. Perhaps in response to Gorbachev, Party Second Secretary Ligachev, speaking a fortnight later on the 69th anniversary of the October Revolution, posed the problem with a slightly different emphasis: 'Peace has become the highest value of humanity, . . . an indispensable condition of its survival. But this does not mean that other realities have retreated into the background'.[25]

The quotation from Lenin to which Gorbachev (and, following him, other commentators[26]) refers is taken from Lenin's notes on the draft programme of the Bolshevik Party, written in 1899 and first published in 1924. Lenin is here recommending that the necessity of the struggle against tsarist autocracy for political freedom be explained as 'not only in the interests of the working class but also in the interests of social development as a whole, . . . for, from the point of view of the basic ideas of Marxism, the interests of social development are higher than the interests of the proletariat'.[27] We see that Gorbachev, in bending the quotation to his purposes, has inserted the phrase 'all-human values', absent in the original, and dubiously implied that Lenin too perceived some conflict between working-class and general social interests.

It is illuminating to view the argument about peace against the background of broader attitudes towards moral values. The official ideology has traditionally been hostile to moral absolutism as subversive of communist morality: all means – or at least all necessary and efficacious means – are justified by the communist end. One author who urged young people to seek the meaning of life in the absolute moral values defended by Dostoevsky and Tolstoy was attacked by *Kommunist* in 1983 for 'abandoning the class approach to morality', and the publication of his book was branded a serious ideological error.[28] On the other hand, since Khrushchev's time it has been widely felt, especially among the intelligentsia, that the moral regeneration of Soviet society requires the recognition of absolute values. This is the central theme of the literature both of Khrushchev's thaw and now of Gorbachev's. Professor Ganchuk, the hero of Yuri Trifonov's *The House on the Embankment*, muses whether the message of Dostoevsky's *Crime and Punishment* – that man needs a line which he is not to cross – is not after all right.[29]

More recently, a literary critic rails against the 'so numerous theoreticians and practitioners of so-called "situational" morality, which permits a person any baseness if it is allowed or, even more so, dictated by the specific circumstances of time and place'.[30] The striving of moral absolutes expresses itself partly in unofficial and semi-official interest in a variety of non-Leninist traditions, from Christianity to Kant's humanism. At the same time, Gorbachev's 'new thinking' has enabled moral absolutism to establish a precarious foothold in the fortress of official ideology.

7
CAPITALISM AND MILITARISM

The identification of socialism with peace and of capitalism with the threat and reality of war underlie the doctrine that peace is strengthened in step with movement of the correlation of forces in favour of socialism. In order to argue that a secure peace is attainable in advance of a further substantial improvement in the correlation of forces, it is necessary to show that capitalism need not inevitably function in a militaristic mode. This means that the thesis of the inherently aggressive 'nature' or 'essence' of imperialism (i.e. the highest, twentieth-century stage of capitalism), which Soviet ideology inherits from Lenin, has to be challenged, or at least reinterpreted in a way that minimizes its practical import.

The 'aggressiveness of imperialism' explained
Six main reasons are adduced for 'the aggressiveness of imperialism', three economic and three political:

(1) the special interests of the Western (primarily American) military-industrial complex;

(2) the role of military expenditure in ameliorating the economic crisis of capitalism;

(3) the function of militarism in protecting the economic interests of imperialism in the Third World against the claims of anti-imperialist forces;

(4) the function of militarism in preserving the world position of capitalism against all forces of social progress;

(5) the function of militarism in obstructing social progress within the imperialist States themselves; and

(6) the generation of militarism by conflicts arising among capitalist States.[1]

Let us survey the debates surrounding each of these factors in turn, and then consider how the issue as a whole relates to the question of the prospects for disarmament.

(1)   The special interests of the military-industrial complex

The military-industrial complex is generally viewed as the central driving-force of capitalist militarism. It stands accused not only of stoking up the arms race in its quest for superprofits, but also of pressing for a more aggressive foreign policy in order to create a political justification for the arms race. But the extent of its ramifications in Western societies and economies, its effect on the functioning of the capitalist economy, and the possibility of its dissolution are all matters of controversy.

Some Soviet analysts advocate a broad, and others a relatively narrow, definition of the military-industrial complex. Those who take the most jaundiced view of the USA, such as Yakovlev, not only regard the complex as including the dominant core of capitalist industry but argue that broad strata of American society are entangled in the net of military-industrial interests.[2] An opposing school of thought, strongly represented in the Institute for the Study of the USA and Canada, holds that:

> although an effort is made to create a 'complex of participation' in the interests of the military-industrial complex among broad strata of Americans, the basic mass of business interests are not and cannot be drawn into the arms race ... The basic interests of the overwhelming majority of US firms depend on mass production for civilian markets, with the normal functioning of which militarization of the economy increasingly clearly interferes ... The policy of recent militaristic US administrations latently but more and more deeply diverges from the basic interests of the business world.[3]

Yuri Zamoshkin, who heads a department studying American public opinion at the USA Institute, has orally criticized Yakovlev for extending attacks on US government policy to include the American people.

A report of an international conference of analysts of contemporary capitalism convened by a multilateral commission of the Academies of Sciences of the socialist countries in East Berlin in November 1985 reveals considerable controversy over the correct conception of the military-industrial complex. Some speakers warned that the growth of militarism in the West is based in the interest of the whole ruling class, and must not be attributed merely to the activity of one particular fraction of it. Others, above all the East Germans, stressed the undesirability of identifying the military-industrial complex with the whole of the State structure and ruling class. It should be treated in a restricted sense as an alliance of armaments firms with the highest military levels of the State apparatus. East German scholars also argued against the view that a specifically West European military-industrial complex has already taken shape.[4] The optimistic stance of the East Germans is comprehensible in the light of the fact that, whereas the Ulbricht leadership was wary of detente, East Germany under Honecker became more deeply committed to detente than the USSR itself.[5]

Within the USSR, however, the proponents of broad definitions remain influential. This is shown by the failure to adopt revisions of the draft of the new Party Programme, proposed at a Party meeting at the Institute of World Economy and International Relations and elsewhere, which were aimed at shifting the focus of condemnation from the Western ruling class as a whole to its militaristic section. The critics had argued that it was wrong to include as parts of the military-industrial complex the whole of the State bureaucracy and of the ideological media, since many State departments lack direct or even indirect connections with the military, and many means of ideological influence do not serve militaristic interests.[6]

The most heterodox of Soviet analysts go beyond arguing over definitions to question the very concept of specifically military-industrial interests. They point out that the typical large Western corporation produces both military and civilian goods (for example, Boeing produces missiles, military and civilian aircraft and also agricultural machinery), flexibly reallocating its capacities in line with sharp fluctuations in military orders. Even the most 'militarized' corporation is sufficiently diversified to be ready for any situation, including the necessity of wholesale conversion to civilian output which would follow disarmament.[7] Of course, such attempts to debunk obsession with the military-industrial complex are susceptible to counter-arguments emphasizing the advantages that firms derive from military production.[8]

(2) The regulatory role of military expenditure

Militarism is explained by some, in particular military, ideologists in terms of efforts by the capitalist State to 'find a way out of the economic crisis of capitalism'. However, the idea that military expenditure can be an effective means of staving off crisis in the capitalist economy has been repeatedly refuted in a large body of Soviet economic literature.[9] While military expenditures are admittedly used to even out cyclical fluctuations, their overall impact is held to be wholly negative. They fuel inflation and, being less labour-intensive, are less effective than civilian expenditures in stimulating employment and final demand. Conversion of military-industrial capacities to civilian output would therefore reduce unemployment and inflation, as well as helping to create a more favourable climate for international trade.

This literature advocating a capitalist economy restored to health through demilitarization has always been in implicit tension with the mainstream of Soviet ideology, which holds that capitalism cannot escape from its state of general crisis. An obvious temptation is to interpret it simply as a contribution to external peace propaganda. However, the genre draws upon research into the mathematical modelling of the capitalist economy which began in the 1960s and continues today. Publication of the results of the early work set off arguments apparently related to their implications for the crisis-free prospects of capitalism.[10]

What might always have been somewhat speculatively read into these economic analyses – that is, that they were intended as contributions to an internal ideological debate – is substantiated by an article entitled 'American corporations and militarism', which appeared in 1986 under the name of I.D. Ivanov, at that time deputy director of the Institute of World Economy and International Relations.[11] The results of the modelling research of the 1960s are here adduced in support of more theoretical considerations to the effect that, far from military production being an 'objectively necessary link in the functioning of the capitalist economy as a whole', it is 'only a derivative, secondary phenomenon'. In fact, from the point of view of the reproduction of capital, it can even be regarded as a phenomenon 'alien' to capitalism, which does not need a parasitic military machine sucking out its juices.[12] As a matter of economic principle, the process of militarization of the economy can be reversed, right up to the point of elimination of the military sector. Ivanov argues further that the 'non-militarized model of capitalist economy' is a real possibility for the future because it already exists 'in a significant group of countries'. The point is also made by Krasin, who names Finland, Austria and Switzerland as examples.

The opposite view, however, is in 1987 still appearing in print in military journals. 'The origin . . . and development of the military-industrial complex of the USA', writes Colonel Petrov in the journal of the Institute of Military History, 'are conditioned by the objective regularities of capitalism.'[13] Similarly, Central Committee official Zagladin declares in the journal of the armed forces' Main Political Administration that 'militarism and the arms race have become an inseparable part of contemporary capitalist society, and to a large extent a condition of its existence.'[14]

Some analysts, such as the former Soviet military technologist Mikhail Agursky, suggest that the Soviet debate about the relationship between militarism and the capitalist economy is a coded debate about the relationship between militarism and the *Soviet* economy.[15] Openly it is always held that there are no really significant obstacles to demilitarization of the Soviet economy, but there is some evidence that certain powerful groups believe that the military competition has a beneficial impact on the economy, in particular by stimulating technical progress. The director and lead actor of a recent Soviet film about an imaginary nuclear crisis, *At the Exit of the Night*, write: 'Today, too, there are people who demonstrate the impossibility of development without wars, which supposedly facilitate progress in technology. The viewer will meet such "theoreticians" in the film.'[16] The debate may therefore concern the relationship between militarism and economic development in both social systems.

(3) *Protection of economic interests in the Third World*
Militarism serves to protect the economic interests of imperialist capital in the Third World – in particular, its capital investments and control over sources of energy and raw materials – against the claims

of anti-imperialist movements and governments. Those who stress this factor argue that the imperialists are not in a position to protect their interests to their satisfaction by non-military means alone, so their resort to a policy of aggression is to be expected. 'In the last decade', explained former Central Committee Secretary K. V. Rusakov to a conference of ideological educators in 1982, 'the strategy of US imperialism to maintain its control [over the Third World] by means of economic pressure and political manoeuvring has failed', and imperialism has accordingly shifted to greater reliance on military means.[17] Gen.-Col. Gareyev warns that, in the face of 'growing contradictions between imperialism and the national-liberation movement, especially with regard to energy resources', imperialism is likely to resort to local wars.[18]

Other analysts of foreign affairs, however, draw attention to the fact that the imperialist States have adapted themselves to some extent to changes in their relations with the Third World. For example, A. Grigorev reports how the capitalist countries have moved towards a more economical use of materials and energy and the recycling of waste products in response to the rise in prices of Third World energy and raw material exports since the beginning of the 1970s.[19] More important is the as yet unused potential for fuller adaptation. In their study of the role of raw materials in international relations, A. Arbatov and A. Shakai argue that the capitalist countries are not in a position to cope with the problem of the dangerous instability of their economic relations with the Third World 'by using the traditional arsenal of means of bourgeois society'. But 'in a long-term perspective' the problem can be successfully resolved in the context of East-West detente, which will make it possible to narrow the gap between rich and poor countries and to develop a reliable, qualitatively new energy and mineral base for the world economy by means of the unified efforts of the industrialized capitalist and socialist States.[20] In general, optimistically declares Georgy Arbatov, director of the USA Institute, 'scientific-technical progress has opened up the opportunities for peacefully solving many of the problems which have often caused wars.'[21]

Another study of relations between the USA and the Third World, that of A.V. Nikiforov, also of the USA Institute, serves to illustrate the sceptical approach taken to such reformist perspectives by the more traditional analysts. Nikiforov regards the idea of a satisfactory compromise between the interests of big capital and those of Third World development as a 'petty-bourgeois illusion'. For the envisaged restriction of neo-colonialist exploitation 'will sooner or later come into contradiction with the class essence of Western States, the policy of which is determined in the first instance by the interests of big capital'. 'It is not by chance', he adds, discounting such Western figures as Brandt and Palme, 'that the liberal and social-reformist advocates [of substantial concessions to the Third World] find themselves in permanent opposition to the governments of Western States.'[22]

The possibility of capitalism reducing reliance upon, and eventually abandoning, its military instrument depends, in general, on its ability to carry through the reforms by which – with some help from socialism – it might reliably manage the problems facing it by peaceful means. The crucial issue is the viability of capitalist reform. Those who deny that reform is feasible have a ready explanation for the current weakness of 'the reform wing of the bourgeoisie': small reforms would solve nothing, while big ones would undermine the capitalist structure by introducing socialist elements into it.[23]

(4)   Preservation of the world position of capitalism

Soviet ideology has traditionally assigned militarism the role of an instrument for preserving and consolidating the world position of capitalism against the natural process of erosion by the forces of social progress, which imperialism strives artificially to stop and reverse. 'Imperialism tries to delay its disappearance and hopes to regain its lost positions by armed force'[24] because, apart from surrender, this is the only strategy open to it: 'Having lost the historical initiative, ... imperialism is no longer in a position to oppose the socialist world with anything other than armed force, the threat of nuclear conflict.'[25]

Against this, Ivanov argues that the 'defensive reaction' of capitalism to the advance of socialism 'may take on various forms, not necessarily military ones';[26] the military reaction is 'by no means inevitable ..., especially given the contemporary strategic situation'.[27] Those who adopt the perspective 'peace first, socialism later' may suppose that the hostility of the West can be placated, at least for a certain period, by an accommodation with capitalist interests. Thus, according to Gavrilov and Patrushev, the way into an era of peaceful relations and cooperation can be opened by means of compromises and 'an extremely agonizing search to combine conflicting aims and interests'.[28]

Many of those wishing to argue the possibility of a demilitarized capitalism seem more at home with economic analysis, and to find the political arguments of their opponents harder to deal with. Rather than tackle the thesis of the unchangeable class hostility of imperialism head on, they try to minimize its implications for the prospects of peace. For example, Krasin grants that 'imperialism remains aggressive in nature' owing to its class enmity towards socialism and the world revolutionary process. However, capitalism should not be considered in the abstract, as if it were 'in some worldwide vacuum'. It is embedded in an international social environment which, thanks to the action of the forces of peace, 'to a growing degree exercises influence on it, right up to the point of modifying the laws of its development'. As a result, the aggressive tendencies of imperialism 'can be, if not blocked, then at least restricted and held in check'.[29]

The problem of the ultimate and irreducible political hostility of the Western ruling class towards socialism has always been the Achilles' heel of ideologists trying to revise the dominant line on capitalism and militarism. Thus one writer on disarmament of the Khrushchev period who asserted that the majority of Western capitalists 'in no way have any interest in the arms race'[30] was criticized in *Kommunist* for 'forgetting the decisive political side of the matter, the fear of the imperialists in the face of socialism, ... which impels [them] to accept certain sacrifices and expenses ... in order to preserve capitalist domination'.[31]

Specific economic arguments for the possibility of a non-militaristic capitalism also evoke specific political counter-arguments. The experience of the small European neutrals may prove that the demilitarization of capitalism is economically feasible, but its political significance can be explained away in terms of a division of functions among capitalist States. At any one time there is always a main adversary which takes on itself the task of defending the long-term interests of capitalism as a historical formation.[32]

An ultimate political argument remains to the optimists. War, now 'as suicidal for capitalism as for socialism, ... has ceased to correspond to the general class interests of the bourgeoisie', though the relative autonomy of militarism enables it 'to defy the broader and longer-term interests of the ruling class as a whole'.[33] The same class instinct of self-preservation which prompts unending attempts to 'throw back' socialism acquires under contemporary conditions a new content and 'begins to work against militarism'.[34]

(5) *The obstruction of social progress internally*

Militarism serves to impede social progress within capitalist States as it does on the international level. A militarist policy controls and diverts social tensions (as in the British-Argentine war on both sides). One of its purposes is to discredit internal progressive forces in the eyes of the masses by identifying them with the alleged threat from without, fear of which is intermittently whipped up into a war psychosis.[35]

The worst Soviet fear is that, in a situation of deepened crisis, capitalism may again give birth to fascism, leading to war. In his Report to the 27th Party Congress, Gorbachev warned of 'the serious danger to international relations of any further substantial shift . . . of the internal situation in some capitalist countries to the right'.[36] The director of the Institute of the International Workers' Movement, T.T. Timofeyev, may be aiming at some Soviet ideologists when he criticizes 'the ultra-pessimistic arguments' of Western leftist writers who allegedly think that the economic crisis of capitalism makes its slide into reaction and war inevitable. Experience shows, he writes, that the political consequences of crisis are indeterminate – some countries may move to the right, others to the left.[37]

The effectiveness of militarism as a brake on internal progress is used to demonstrate the necessity of the 'peace first, socialism later' strategy. Central Committee Secretary Dobrynin argues that shifts to the left in the capitalist countries are at present impeded because 'the very situation of international confrontation evokes and stimulates chauvinist moods, pushing part of the working class to the right, even the extreme right.' The demilitarization of international relations is accordingly 'the main fundamental precondition for success in solving the social problems facing the working class'.[38]

(6) *Inter-capitalist conflicts*

Lenin's theory of imperialist militarism drew primarily on the experience of inter-imperialist conflict in the First World War rather than on that of capitalist-socialist conflict in the War of Intervention. Even in the Stalin period, the crucial component of the then dominant doctrine of the inevitability of war concerned inter-imperialist war.[39] It is only since the 1950s that Soviet ideologists have viewed conflicts between capitalist States as overshadowed by the central contest between the capitalist and socialist blocs, although some such conflicts continue to bear the seeds of war (e.g. that between Greece and Turkey).

How real a danger may still be presented by the possible future remilitarization of inter-imperialist contradictions is a matter of dispute. Shakhnazarov does not rule out a revival of German or Japanese militarism.[40] For an optimistic observer like Bovin, on the other hand, 'the probability of wars between imperialist powers at the end of the twentieth century is practically equal to zero.'[41]

Capitalist militarism and the prospects for disarmament

There has always been a striking discordance between public Soviet proposals for drastic measures of disarmament and the Soviet characterization of the capitalist system as inherently militaristic. Indeed, we know from the correspondence between Lenin and his foreign minister, Chicherin, in preparation for the Genoa Conference of 1922 that the practice was established at that time of deliberately publicizing disarmament proposals for propaganda purposes in the full expectation that they would not be accepted by the capitalist States.[42]

Khrushchev attempted to reconcile his campaign for general and complete disarmament with the thesis of the aggressiveness of imperialism by maintaining that, although the threat of war would last as long as capitalism, it was possible to pit against the forces of war a yet greater force for peace. The socialist countries had acquired the means to influence or 'even compel' the capitalist States to agree to disarmament.[43] The same basic argument has been used repeatedly since: the forces of peace can 'counteract', 'neutralize', 'restrict' or 'keep in check' the aggressive strivings of imperialism and thereby bring about disarmament.[44] Most recently, Alexander Bovin has explained that nuclear disarmament, as proposed by Gorbachev, is 'a difficult task [but] possible in principle in the late twentieth century' because the nature of capitalism, still militaristic from an abstract point of view, cannot but be influenced by the practical circumstances of the nuclear age. 'The "nature" itself does not change. But the mechanism of its realization does change.'[45]

The theory that a tiger can be securely tamed while its dangerous essence remains intact has about it something of a scholastic air. If we are to accept the testimony of the defector Arkady Shevchenko, Khrushchev did not take seriously his own theory. In 1959 Khrushchev told Shevchenko that, in contrast to real negotiations on limited steps of arms control, the campaign for general and complete disarmament was a propaganda instrument. Khrushchev admitted that he neither expected the West to disarm completely nor contemplated such a course for the Soviet Union.[46] In his own memoirs, on the other hand, Khrushchev expressed the hope that general and complete disarmament would in the long term prove attainable.[47]

Again, in 1971, when Shevchenko suggested to his superior Gromyko that the USSR propose a conference of the five nuclear powers to consider nuclear disarmament, he discovered that top officials were opposed to complete nuclear disarmament as a goal. While their real concern was to retain for the USSR the status of a nuclear power, the legitimizing function of the ideological thesis of 'the aggressive nature of imperialism' is shown by Minister of Defence Grechko's use of it to justify his sceptical stance towards the proposed conference.[48]

There are indications in the Soviet literature as well that the power elite has not on the whole expected the radical demilitarization of East-West relations. The fifty-year forecasts which Central Committee official Shakhnazarov made in the late 1970s list 'complete nuclear disarmament' and 'abolition of the military-industrial complex of imperialism' under the heading 'zero probability'.[49]

The announcement of Gorbachev's plan for complete nuclear disarmament by the year 2000 has been followed by the publication of several articles defending the plan's feasibility. One can regard the articles of Ivanov and Krasin at the beginning of 1986, and those of Bovin and Arbatov at the beginning of 1987, in this light. Bovin takes issue with unidentified internal 'sceptics' who consider the Gorbachev proposal 'a utopia, useful as a propaganda act but impossible as a political solution'. The objections and doubts of the sceptics are both 'of a general historical and philosophical character' (the militaristic nature of capitalism) and strategic (the unreliability of purely conventional deterrence and the danger of secret nuclear rearmament).[50]

Bovin grants the abstract correctness of the traditional thesis of the aggressive nature of capitalism, merely questioning its practical import. Ivanov, however, makes a political attack on the thesis itself. The error of falsely elevating militarism from a parasitic phenomenon into 'an inevitable stage in the development of capitalism ... means putting in doubt the possibility of stopping the arms race and of disarmament, and in the final analysis also the possibility of preventing nuclear conflict'. Moreover, he asserts, 'the peace-loving foreign policy of the Soviet Union follows from' the possibility that capitalism will undergo a process of demilitarization.[51] By implication, the foreign policy associated with the traditional thesis is *not* peace-loving. Similarly, Krasin condemns the 'deeply pessimistic' position which 'takes the achievement of a stable peace beyond the bounds of the present epoch, affirming in essence the futility of current efforts to secure it'.[52]

The impression which emerges is of a division between traditionalists, for whom Gorbachev's scheme for nuclear disarmament is (like simiiar schemes in the past) no more than propaganda, and representatives of 'the new thinking', presumably including Gorbachev himself, who seriously pursue the goal of elimination of nuclear weapons. Of course, it is conceivable that the creation of this impression is itself just a more elaborate form of propaganda. However, the fact that the main ideological thesis which has legitimized a cynical approach to the disarmament issue is now a matter of dispute should alert us to the possibility that a historic shift in the Soviet Union may be under way.

8
INTERDEPENDENCE AND GLOBAL PROBLEMS

In recent years, especially under Gorbachev, Soviet ideology has increasingly stressed the growing 'interdependence', 'interconnectedness' and 'wholeness' of the world, while simultaneously pointing out its diversity and antagonisms.[1] The main components of interdependence are enumerated thus by Gorbachev: 'Our world is united not only by the internationalization of economic life and by powerful information and communications media but also in facing the common danger of nuclear death, ecological catastrophe and global explosion of the contradictions between its poor and wealthy regions.'[2]

There are two distinct though overlapping strands here: recognition of the functional integration of the world economy and of world communications, and concern with 'global problems' that threaten the future of humanity and require international cooperation for their solution.

We first trace how the concept of 'global problems' has emerged and been defined in the USSR, and consider the impact that the existence of global problems is held to have on world politics. Then we survey the debate on economic interdependence.

Emergence of the concept of 'global problems'
Soviet 'globalistics' seems to have originated during the 1970s in attempts to emulate the global modelling projections of the Club of Rome and similar research groups in the West. These attempts

apparently met obstruction from scholars and officials who 'under-estimated the great importance of the deeper development of research in the field'. The Western inspiration of the work aroused suspicions of ideological unsoundness: globalistics was felt to ignore the struggle between capitalism and socialism, and was associated with the taboo idea of convergence between the systems.[3] Neverthe-less, the concept of 'global problems' won increasing high-level support. Global problems were mentioned by Brezhnev in his Report to the 25th Party Congress in 1976, and reference to them has now been included in the new Party Programme.[4]

By the beginning of the 1980s, global modelling had acquired considerable organizational backing. The two main centres of work were the Institute of World Economy and International Relations, with groups working on different global problems (energy, raw materials, food, ecology, underdevelopment, etc.) within a continu-ing research programme,[5] and the All-Union Scientific Research Institute for Systems Investigations, where members of the 'global project' team, directed by Academician Gvishiani, study global problems by means of theoretical and applied computer models.[6] Western research was being monitored by a working group at the USA Institute. Coordination was provided by a section for global problems of the Academy of Sciences' Scientific Council on the Philosophical and Social Problems of Science and Technology, headed by Academician Frolov.[7]

Three figures have played key parts in ideologically legitimizing the concept of global problems. Its main patron in the Party apparatus has been the deputy head of the International Depart-ment, Vadim Zagladin, who has written the most authoritative articles on the question. Frolov, a prominent philosopher recently appointed editor of *Kommunist*, has been especially concerned with the ecological theme. Gvishiani, who in addition to his Soviet posts chairs the Council of the International Institute of Applied Systems Analysis at Vienna, has developed the 'systems approach'.[8]

These writers have established Marxist credentials for the 'all-human approach', in particular by reference to the humanist con-cepts of the early Marx, such as 'the species-being of humanity'. These concepts had previously been 'treated as abstractions', while the practical stress had been laid on the 'class approach'.[9] Global problems cannot, as 'some comrades' suggest, be viewed purely as an expression of the contradiction between socialism and capitalism because, though capitalism is the main culprit, socialism is not free of all of them (the production process gives rise to ecological problems, for example, in any society) and shares responsibility for their solution.[10]

However, the expositions of globalistics produced by the more prominent ideologists were aimed simultaneously at the legitimation of the field and at the imposition upon it of what they considered necessary ideological constraints. Both sides of the earlier controversies were reproved: the conservative opponents of globalistics for being 'insufficiently aware of the nature and depth of the influence of global problems on the life and development of humanity', and its advocates for taking an uncritical attitude towards Western work.[11] The all-human approach was to complement, not supersede, the class approach. The crucial constraining thesis stated that, while international cooperation to *tackle* global problems must not be delayed, it is only when the whole world is socialist that it will become possible optimally to *solve* the problems.[12] Moreover, in the meantime global problems are a sphere of competition as well as cooperation between the systems.[13]

The lists of global problems given by different authors show a certain amount of variation. However, the problem of war and peace always comes first as the most vital and urgent of global problems. Next come various problems relating to the ecological situation, resources and underdevelopment: defence of the natural environment, the secure long-term provision and rational management of energy, food and raw materials (including exploitation of the world ocean), the economic and cultural backwardness of developing countries (including hunger, disease, illiteracy and demographic problems). Finally, mention may be made of the use of outer space, and of shared problems in such fields as health-care, education, culture and urbanization (e.g. securing 'human integrity').[14]

Since the identification of a given problem as a global one by definition implies the need for international cooperation in tackling it, arguments about which problems are to be considered global are of more than academic significance. As Zagladin observes, three usages are to be found in the Soviet literature. At one extreme, only those problems are admitted as global which pose a clear threat to human survival. At the other, 'practically all problems generated by human activity' and for which international cooperation might prove useful are counted as global problems.

Zagladin favours a definition of intermediate scope. He suggests that global problems have two distinguishing characteristics: first, 'they involve the interests of the whole of humanity ... They affect the fate of people now living and of future generations ... They are in essence the long-term problems of future humanity. In this sense ... global problems are *all-human* in nature.' Second, 'their solution as a rule requires a deep qualitative transformation of all spheres of social activity ... and some change in the system of social priorities, ... not enclosed within national boundaries, a fundamental reconstruction of international relations.'[15]

The concept of global problems used by Gorbachev is strikingly broad. In his Prague speech of April 1987, he states that 'dozens of problems are becoming global', and calls for cooperation against AIDS, terrorism, crime and drug addiction as well as against the war danger, underdevelopment and pollution.[16]

A feature of much Soviet writing on global problems is the salience of the ecological theme. The anxiety about environmental collapse is in sharp contrast to previously dominant Soviet positions on the relationship between Man and Nature. Academician Frolov in particular emphasizes that 'ecological thinking' is an essential component of the 'all-human global thinking' which is needed.[17]

Lastly, we should note that Soviet globalistics lays great stress on the close synergistic interaction of the main global problems. This requires that a systems approach be adopted to their analysis.[18] In this respect also, the key problem is always held to be that of war and peace. The arms race endangers humanity not only as a result of the direct threat of war it entails, but also because it wastes resources (including scarce metals) needed to tackle ecological and development problems, thereby generating additional indirect threats of war. Conversely, disarmament could open the way to cooperative efforts against the other global dangers before it is too late.[19]

The impact of global problems on world politics

The growing interdependence of the world, as the philosopher Academician Ursul argues, requires

> a new, global social consciousness, the reorientation of the thinking of politicians and strategists, responsible now no longer only for the fate of their own countries, but also for that

of all humanity. In solving the internal problems of one or another country, including problems of security, the problems of other States can no longer be ignored.[20]

Many Soviet ideologists perceive that this global consciousness is indeed arising. Some, like Grigoryan, see the roots of global consciousness in a wide range of 'unifying tendencies of world development': modern transport, intensive economic, political and cultural interchange, and the broad diffusion of information on world events through the mass media have 'made the globe accessible and perceptible' to enormous numbers of people.[21] But it is the 'community of fate of all peoples, ... the situation ... in which various social systems can either survive or perish only together', imposed on the human race by its global problems, which is assigned the main role in generating 'an increasingly clear self-perception of humanity as a single, though contradictory, whole'.[22] To the traditional categories of international relations such as national, State and class interests, argue Tomashevsky and Lukov, is now added the category of 'interests of humanity'. There appears a crucial new division in world politics, that between those who do and those who do not understand the need to give priority to common human interests. Moreover, 'the dividing line in this struggle does not usually run between classes and parties but within them'.[23]

Assertions of this kind, in according primacy to ideas, appear hard to reconcile with Marxian materialism. Advocates of the all-human approach, however, insist that their approach remains a fully materialist one. In analysing the determinants of historical events, Marxism has traditionally concentrated on the forces and relations of production and the class struggles associated with them. But this class approach, which implicitly takes continued human survival as a given, is no longer adequate in the age of global problems. The analyst cannot now be satisfied with the twofold Marxist distinction between the political and cultural 'superstructure' of society and its productive 'base', but must dig deeper to take proper account of the 'sub-base' of biological conditions of human existence:

In his time, Engels ... stressed 'the simple fact that people must first of all eat, drink, have shelter and clothing before they are in a position to occupy themselves with politics, science, art, religion, etc.'. Today, one might add to this that before eating,

drinking, having shelter and clothing, people must first of all
secure the preservation of the human race ... The solution of
all other questions – economic, social, political, ideological, etc.
– depends on this.[24]

In the past, Marxists regarded talk of the unity of interests of
humanity as 'impractical idealism or political romanticism',
infinitely removed from the social reality of class and other antagonisms. But now 'the threat of general annihilation [has] cast doubt on
the idea of the divisibility of the fates of different nations ... in the
event of war, [and] given rise to a "global" consciousness speaking
"in the name of humanity".' The social significance of humanistic
appeals, writes L. Mitrokhin of the Institute of the International
Workers' Movement, is essentially changed: 'It is as if they have
been brought down to earth, more and more compellingly seen as
practical and urgent.'[25]

The unified consciousness of common interests develops in
conflict and interaction with the pre-existing divided consciousness
of opposed interests. In the words of O.N. Melikyan (of the same
Institute), 'The working-out of the new world-perception of human
unity ... proceeds in the presence of social, class, ideological,
political, national and State ... contradictions and conflicts ... All
these contradictions are not abolished by awareness of the nuclear
threat, but they cannot but be modified by it.'[26]

The rise of global consciousness is a new factor working in favour
of detente, the basis of which ceases to be 'a temporary, partial
coincidence of interests' and becomes instead 'the objective long-
term common interest' in human survival.[27] The crucial issue here,
from the point of view of Soviet ideology, is the rate at which global
consciousness can be expected to permeate the Western ruling class.
The more optimistic ideologists, such as Central Committee con-
sultant Yuri Zhilin, do indeed claim to detect a gradual rise in the
global awareness of the capitalist class.[28]

It is, however, now admitted that Soviet thinking too needs to be
adapted to the requirements of global consciousness. Central Committee Secretary Dobrynin called in 1986 for efforts 'further to
develop and enrich' Marxism-Leninism by combining it with 'the
humanistic and general democratic ideals of all social forces
seriously concerned for the self-preservation of humanity'.[29] This is
the ideological counterpart to the political strategy of building a

broad united front of communists, social-democrats, liberals, religious people and moderate conservatives against the nuclear threat embodied in 'the most reactionary circles of imperialism', often compared to the anti-fascist united front of the 1930s and 1941–5.[30]

The debate on economic interdependence

Recent years have seen a wide-ranging and complex debate in Soviet journals of economics and international relations on the relationships among national, bloc and world economies. Focusing only on the East-West dimension of the debate, one can distinguish three broad positions:

(a) According to some economists, such as Academician G. Sorokin, a department head at the Institute of Economics, the capitalist and socialist world-systems are economically 'incompatible and antagonistic'. They cannot form a unity or share a common basis: in fact, their development only deepens the opposition between them.[31] In policy terms, this position advocates minimizing the dependence of the USSR on economic ties with the capitalist world.

(b) An intermediate position, taken by some members of the Institute of World Economy and International Relations, recognizes that there is a growing interdependence between the capitalist and socialist world-systems, which together may be said to comprise the 'macrosystem' of an all-world economy. However, intra-bloc relations are still regarded as primary; the all-world economy 'is not a real organic economy but a sterilized theoretical abstract'. The socio-economic opposition of the two systems sets objective limits to interdependence, and 'practice shows that failure to observe these limits has serious economic and political consequences'[32] (a reference perhaps to such problems as Polish indebtedness).

(c) The most radical position does regard the all-world economy as a single organic whole. In an article appearing in late 1986, Bunkina and Petrov (of the Institute of World Economy and International Relations) define it as 'that economic system in which there takes place the reproduction of the total social product of the planet earth, within which the world-socialist and world-capitalist economies interact'. They criticize the narrow approach of the textbooks used to train foreign-policy and foreign-trade officials, based on the concept of two distinct world economies, socialist and capitalist, the relations between which are of secondary significance. There is only *one* world economy, governed by the action of general economic laws shared by its two component social systems. Economic interaction between socialism and capitalism is not confined, as usually assumed, to the peripheral sphere of trade, viewed as a residual element, but penetrates the whole process of production and reproduction. Socialist countries use imported capital equipment, borrow techniques of industrial management from capitalist business, take part in scientific-technical cooperation, international standardization and so on. Some socialist countries set up joint capitalist-socialist enterprises.[33] (This was before the USSR announced its intention to encourage joint enterprise.) The analysis not only describes but implicitly legitimizes such activities.

This theory of 'interdependence' is really concerned primarily with the continuing dependence of the USSR on world capitalism. It is recalled that Lenin assigned an important role to foreign capitalist concessions during the New Economic Policy in the 1920s, admitting that the Soviet Union needed capitalist help and would have to pay for it. The implication is that the USSR remains in this situation today. The disadvantages of dependence on the world capitalist economy, such as a certain disturbing impact on the Soviet economy of its market fluctuations, just have to be accepted.[34] For, as Burlatsky remarked in a coded reform manifesto in 1982, 'any economy in our time, if it wants to be at a contemporary level, cannot develop without the closest economic ties with the economies of other countries, without participation in the international economic division of labour.'[35]

The application of the concept of the all-world economy to the special case of East-West-South relations has been examined by Elizabeth Valkenier. She shows that the USSR has not managed to escape dependence on the West in its economic relations with the Third World by creating an autonomous East-South economic system. Even Soviet allies of 'socialist orientation' continue to be dependent on ties with the capitalist world. Soviet theorists of interdependence therefore advocate the necessity of trilateral economic cooperation between the developed capitalist and socialist countries and the underdeveloped countries.[36]

The main concerns of the debate on economic interdependence are with economic and technological development as conventionally conceived in a 'pre-globalist' framework. Nevertheless, there are some important links between this debate and the theme of 'global problems'. First of all, as we saw in Chapter 7, the amelioration of global problems such as the development of new sources of energy and raw materials is regarded as one of the fields ripe for East-West (and East-West-South) cooperation.[37] A key part of Ivanov's argument for the possibility of the demilitarization of capitalism is that joint efforts by 'Western corporations and socialist enterprises . . . for the solution of many national and global problems [is] the alternative to military business, both in production and in research.'[38]

A more general consideration is that economic interdependence, whatever its other motivations, 'strengthens the material bases of the peaceful living-together of States and peoples by contributing to an atmosphere of trust and by compelling the aggressive circles of the imperialist States to avoid military conflict. It is precisely . . . the necessity of human survival . . . which requires the stimulation of all kinds of relations between States of the opposing social systems, including economic ties.'[39]

Although it is never denied that economic ties work in favour of peace, it is not universally accepted that they are a factor so decisive as to constitute the material basis of peaceful coexistence. Shakhnazarov, under the guise of a critique of the functionalist school in Western political science, argues that those who rely on the development of economic relations for securing peace 'ignore the factor of time'. He assumes that the integration of the world economy is inevitably a slow, long-term process, not likely soon to yield great political benefits:

One may of course think that the gradual expansion of economic ties will at some time or other lead to the formation of international structures which will secure the future of the world community. But given the present tempo of the arms race and the rate of exacerbation of global problems, humanity simply cannot permit itself to sit with arms crossed, wholly entrusting itself to evolution.[40]

During the debate on the draft new Party Programme, something of a campaign emerged to have the category of the 'all-world economy' incorporated into the draft. The question was raised in the Party press, and Party meetings both at the Institute of World Economy and International Relations and at the Central Committee Institute of Social Sciences called for inclusion of the expression in order 'further to strengthen the theoretical basis of the conception of peaceful coexistence'. The Institute of Social Sciences proposed the sentence: 'The objective economic basis of peaceful coexistence is the all-world economy, the international division of labour.'[41] The continuing influence of opponents of the interdependence perspective is shown by the failure of this campaign to achieve its object.

9

WHITHER THE CORRELATION OF FORCES?

Substitutes or complements?
It is the contention of this study that the new tendency in Soviet ideology to a large degree replaces improvement in the correlation of forces as the material basis of Soviet security by the growth of interdependence. It may be objected that the importance of the correlation of forces has not been clearly repudiated, and that interdependence and the correlation of forces might better be regarded as complementary factors of security: that is, improvement in either factor, other things being equal, is welcomed as advantageous.

I should first explain that the shift as I perceive it has definite limits: it is hardly to be expected that the concept of 'correlation of forces' will disappear from Soviet ideology. What I am arguing is that *substantial improvements* in the correlation of forces, especially in its *military* dimension, are no longer judged essential *for the attainment of a secure peace*. The correlation of forces therefore retains its significance in the following respects:

(a)   It may not be urgent to improve the correlation of forces, but this does not mean that a significant deterioration would be tolerable. No level of interdependence would reconcile the USSR to a position of decisive strategic inferiority vis-à-vis the USA.

(b)   The stress on interdependence is accompanied by emphasis on the importance for peace of improving the economic and other internal dimensions of the correlation of forces, rather than its military dimension.

(c)   As world socialism, and not simply peace, remains the ultimate Soviet goal, the correlation of forces will continue to be an indicator of progress towards this goal, though the weight of its non-military components will increase. But improvement in the correlation of forces for *this* purpose is not such an urgent priority.

Within these limits, I would maintain that the downgrading in importance of the correlation of forces, although not made explicit, is inherent in the logic of the new ideological tendency. This logic can perhaps best be traced in Gorbachev's quite complex treatment of the prospects for peace in his Report to the 27th Party Congress in 1986.[1]

His argument proceeds through several phases. First of all, the militaristic nature of imperialism is declared in no uncertain terms: 'The intrinsic mainsprings and socio-economic essence of imperialism prompt it to translate the competition of the two systems into the language of military confrontation'. Moreover, as the decay of capitalism deepens, so do the chances of a turn away from a militaristic policy decrease: 'The ruling circles do not wish soberly to assess world realities. . . All this is an indicator of the wearing-out of the internal "immune systems" [of capitalism], of its social decrepitude, which reduce the probability of big changes in the policy of the ruling forces and heighten its irrationality.'

Gorbachev here appears to come close to concluding that the most likely prospect is one of rising tension or even war. However, a favourable outcome is possible, depending on the correlation of forces on the world scene, the growth and effectiveness of the peace potential, and the degree of realism achieved by Western ruling circles. These are the traditional underlying factors of peaceful coexistence, but there is a new lack of confidence in their efficacy: 'It is not easy at all, in the current circumstances, to predict the future of [East-West] relations.' The perspective at this point is indeterminate.

But, continues Gorbachev, such indeterminacy is philosophically impermissible to a communist. Some way to the right answer must be found:

Will the ruling centres of capital be able to step on to the path
of sober, constructive assessment of events? Easiest would be to
answer – maybe yes, and maybe no. But history does not give
us the right to such a forecast. We cannot take 'no' as an
answer to the question: Is humanity to be or not to be? We say:
Social progress, the life of civilization, must and will continue.

The prolonged applause that greets this voluntaristic outburst
notwithstanding, Gorbachev recognizes that 'the optimism usual for
communists' serves as an inadequate foundation for forecasting a
happy future. Weighing up the various factors traditionally cited as
working for and against peace has left the outcome still hanging in
the balance, so a new factor is needed to tip the scales in favour of
peace.

And Gorbachev proceeds to introduce the new factor – namely,
'the growing tendency towards interdependence' of the countries of
the world community: 'The need to resolve the most vital problems
affecting all humanity must prompt [the two worlds] towards
interaction, awaken humanity's heretofore unseen powers of self-
preservation.' Interdependence supplies 'the requisite political,
social and material premises' for the global cooperation that is
needed.

The speech does not set out a fully consistent position, and might
best be read as an open-ended thinking-through of the contradictions in which the traditional ideology based on the correlation of
forces has become entangled. The concept of interdependence then
appears as the pointer towards a new position which is still in the
process of being worked out.

The impact of interdependence on the correlation of forces
The level of interdependence and the correlation of forces are not
necessarily independent variables, and some light may be cast on the
meaning of the ideological shift by considering how Soviet ideologists might conceive of the likely impact of growing interdependence on the correlation of forces between socialism and
capitalism.

The mutual vulnerability of interdependence does not, of course,
necessarily constrain both sides to the same degree, nor need the
benefits and costs of cooperation be equally shared. Estimating the

net effect of a given type of interdependence on the correlation of forces in its many dimensions is inevitably a very complex and uncertain exercise. Different criteria may point in opposite directions. For example, the Soviet bloc may derive a greater relative technological benefit from East-West trade, but by the same token it may become more vulnerable to political pressure as its development plans come to depend more heavily on links with the capitalist world.

From the ideological point of view, the *forms* that cooperation takes are in themselves of some importance. Commercial cooperation with Western firms, however advantageous economically, entails an ideological loss. In seeking integration into the capitalist-dominated world economy, the USSR retreats ideologically, confessing the failure of its attempt to build up an independent 'socialist' system of international economic relations and reconciling itself to participation in an institutional framework not influenced by itself.

On the other hand, Soviet ideologists tend to interpret non-commercial forms of cooperation, such as the programmes of the World Health Organization[2] and other UN agencies, as incipiently or in principle 'socialist'. International planning to tackle global problems is seen as to some extent analogous to planning in socialist countries, and as a step towards the eventual creation of a world-wide system of socialist planning after the world victory of socialism.[3] It is in this sense, for example, that one might understand Gorbachev's call for natural resources to be conserved by the setting-up of 'effective international procedures and mechanisms which would make for the rational use of the world's resources as assets belonging to all humanity', so that their use would no longer be subordinated to the blind play of market forces.[4]

Although cooperation may affect the correlation of forces one way or the other, it is also viewed as serving to strengthen *both* systems simultaneously. East-West relations are not a zero-sum game. Thus the publicist Alexander Bovin makes the point that the economic relations of the USSR with West Germany, France and Finland hardly weaken the capitalist system in these countries. It is 'a paradox of our age' that 'irreconcilable systems are historically compelled to cooperate and strengthen one another in order to survive and continue with their dispute'.[5] This is a disturbing thought for minds of a traditional bent. Vadim Zagladin (Central Committee International Department) writes that in one of the letters received by me the view is expressed that the participation of the USSR in international cooperation is in effect 'concern' for monopoly capital. 'May it live and thrive. We shall create heavenly conditions for it.' This approach is fundamentally wrong. In advocating the necessity of broad international cooperation, our Party is concerned not for monopoly capital but for the future of all humanity, including that part of it living under socialism. In our time, in conditions of the growing interdependence of countries, isolation in one's own shell, refusal to take account of the interests and needs of all humanity, are fraught with serious mistakes and dangers.[6]

The misgiving of Zagladin's correspondent – i.e., that the USSR, by pursuing economic cooperation, is helping to stave off the economic crisis of capitalism – is dealt with more directly by the globalists of the Institute of World Economy and International Relations, who argue that 'Marxists ... do not have an interest in the economic crises of capitalism' because these crises are passed on to the developing countries, impede East-West economic relations and endanger peace.[7]

Non-military components of the correlation of forces
In assessing ideological change, we need to gauge not only the relative salience of the general concept of 'correlation of forces' but also the relative stress placed on its various components – military, political, economic and ideological. While all these components were recognized as significant in the 1970s, the military component was clearly assigned a central role as the decisive guarantee of detente. Under Gorbachev, however, analysts have re-emphasized the 'multidimensionality' of the correlation of forces and the limited benefits to be gained from military strength when combined with socio-economic weakness.

In 1985 Professor V.P. Lukin, head of a sector at the USA Institute, set out this argument, using 'the correlation of forces between the USA and Japan' as a foil for the correlation of forces between the USSR and the West:

It is unrealistic to attempt to secure one's own 'absolute security' at the cost of others, ignoring their interests. In our time, the attempt to build one's strategy on the principle of having as much as all the others and a little more is not only unrealizable in practice but even counterproductive. It leads to the overextension of forces and the consequent loss of positions to rivals who have managed to allocate their resources more rationally, taking more sober account of contemporary reality. Look: Japan has spent substantially less on defence than the USA. But has the correlation of forces between these countries really changed proportionally in favour of Washington over recent decades? Quite the contrary! ... Strengthening of the positions of a country in the world and the growth of military expenditure are by no means one and the same.[8]

According to Gorbachev, it was the socio-economic weakness of the USSR at the end of the Brezhnev era that, in spite of the country's military power, tempted the USA to return to a strategy of confrontation: 'Comrades, today we know and understand full well that the all-out offensive ... launched by the forces of reaction at the end of the 1970s and the beginning of the 1980s was brought about by, among other things, our internal state of affairs.'[9] That is, it was the non-military components of the correlation of forces which proved to be decisive. Furthermore, the arms race imposed on the USSR has a socio-economic purpose no less important than the military one – 'to exhaust the Soviet Union economically, ... to hamper the implementation of our social programme and to prevent us from carrying out our reform plans'.[10] It follows that the USSR must protect its socio-economic development by restricting its own military countermeasures to the minimum consistent with averting US strategic superiority. The USA should not 'count on inducing us to make needless expenditures'.[11] We may recall that Khrushchev used the same argument, explaining the drastic reductions he made in the armed forces by his desire 'not to give our adversary the opportunity to exhaust us economically'.[12]

10

ASSESSMENT OF POLITICAL WEIGHTS

So far we have been studying the *content* of Soviet foreign-policy ideology as it has changed since the 1970s. We turn our attention now to the change over time in the relative political strength of the ideological tendencies we have identified.

We begin by analysing various kinds of text. First, the situations in the 1970s, the early 1980s and the period under Gorbachev to date are compared on the basis of the middle-level journal articles and books relied upon in this study. Next we consider the changing content of the Party slogans issued for the anniversary of the October Revolution between 1982 and 1986. The new Party Programme adopted by the 27th Congress in March 1986 is then examined. Lastly, we note positions taken in speeches and articles by members of the present top leadership team with responsibilities in the field of East-West relations.

We also review the evidence of recent personnel appointments and institutional changes within the Soviet foreign-policy establishment. The political weight of ideological tendencies is assessed as of March 1987.

Textual analyses

(*a*) *Middle-level articles and books*
The orthodoxy of the 1970s, described in Chapter 4, has given way in the 1980s to the various perspectives discussed in Chapter 5. How

has the political status of the four main tendencies of the 1980s evolved?

Interruption perspectives, in which short-term pessimism is combined with faith in return at some future time to the high-road to peace and socialism, have been espoused by some prominent figures, notably by Yakovlev, who has been brought into the top leadership under Gorbachev. Recent texts (for example, articles by Zagladin) suggest that this tendency remains an important one.

Fluctuation perspectives, which look to a future changing in a capricious and unpredictable way, have also been put forward by quite prominent Party ideologists. Continuing fluctuations are also expected by military writers, though within relatively narrow bounds. This tendency too is a persistent one.

Confrontation perspectives, in which the intensification of East-West confrontation has now become the dominant historical trend, have been intermittently proclaimed, mainly by certain publicists, though also by some Party ideologists. Articles with this orientation have tended to appear during intervals when East-West relations have been at their most tense – for example, in the early months of 1984. Even at these times, however, the prophets of confrontation have been opposed by more sanguine voices. Confrontation perspectives are only occasionally voiced under Gorbachev (for example, by the writer Prokhanov).

Most crucial is the changing position of the interdependence perspective. In order to assess this, the characteristics of sixteen articles which seemed significant expressions of this perspective were analysed.[1] Their distribution over time was as follows: published in 1982–3, four; published in 1984–5, four; published in 1986 and the first quarter of 1987, eight. That is, articles which separate the struggle for peace from the struggle for socialism first make their appearance in the early 1980s, and the rate at which they appear sharply increases under Gorbachev. Moreover, the recent articles are much more explicit, fairly clearly spelling out what had to be indirectly inferred from earlier articles.

Most important of all, the median status of the authors of 'interdependence' articles is much higher in the recent period. So is the status of the journals in which several of them appear. The earlier articles were written by scholars and publicists not enjoying very great prominence, and published mainly in journals associated with institutes of the Academy of Sciences. Some of the authors of the later articles are prominent academic and Party figures, and some of the most significant articles appear in such authoritative Party outlets as *Pravda* and *Kommunist*. (The appointment of Frolov to replace the more confrontationist Kosolapov as editor of *Kommunist* may be pertinent.) One straw in the wind is the shift in position of the senior ideologist Krasin, evident in comparing articles of his published in 1981 and 1986.[2]

However, while the interdependence perspective has now acquired a political status roughly on the level of other influential perspectives, it is as yet far from constituting a new orthodoxy. Texts in clear discord with it have appeared even quite recently. A 1986 book on peace ideology by M.I. Basmanov, for instance, stresses the inseparability of the struggles for peace and for social progress, and argues that particular partial changes are quite probable, but radical transformations of the foreign policy of capitalist States are impossible while the basis of society remains capitalist: 'wars will end with the departure of capitalism and the arrival of socialism.'[3]

The writing of military ideologists also only quite tenuously reflects ideas from the interdependence perspective. Thus Col.-Gen. Professor D.A. Volkogonov of the Main Political Administration repeatedly asserts that 'we must achieve full economic independence from the capitalist countries, which often try to use the sphere of trade and economic cooperation for purposes of pressure and blackmail.'[4]

The foreign-affairs institutes of the Academy of Sciences may on the whole be regarded as institutional strongholds of the interdependence perspective. For example, the Institute of World Economy and International Relations is, as we have seen, closely associated with concepts like the integration of the world economy and the viability of a demilitarized model of capitalism. On the other hand, even in these institutes more traditional approaches are by no means absent: the attack on 'interdependence', as applied in particular to West-South relations, by A.V. Nikiforov of the USA Institute may be recalled (Chapter 7).

(*b*) *Anniversary slogans*

A set of several dozen official slogans[5] is published in *Pravda* each year for use in the celebrations of the anniversary of the October Revolution, and comparison of the slogans issued in different years throws some light on the changing priorities of Party policy. Study of the foreign-policy slogans over the five-year period 1982–6 shows striking changes from 1984 onwards.[6]

We might first note the introduction into the slogans of the theme of international cooperation, absent (except in the context of intra-bloc relations) up to 1983. From 1984, the lead foreign-policy slogan 'Hail to the Soviet Union's peace-loving Leninist foreign policy!' is extended into 'Hail to the Soviet Union's Leninist foreign policy – a policy of strengthening peace and the security of peoples, of broad international cooperation!'

Moreover, in 1986 'cooperation' gets two more mentions, in the new slogan 'People of the world! Step up the struggle for the improvement of the international situation and constructive cooperation among States!' and in a call for 'security and coopera-tion in the Asian-Pacific region' (the theme of Asian security having been introduced in 1985).

At the same time, there is between 1982 and 1986 a dramatic decline in the theme of anti-imperialist struggle. Up to 1982 there are many separate slogans of solidarity with the liberation struggles of particular Third World countries (Afghanistan, Angola, Chile, El Salvador, etc.). In 1983–5 there is a considerable reduction in the number of solidarity slogans, and they no longer relate to individual countries. In 1986, only one portmanteau slogan devoted to the anti-imperialist theme survives, and its emphasis is on the resolution of regional conflicts rather than on struggle ('Against imperialist aggression, eliminate tension and crisis situations in Asia, Africa and Latin America!').

(c) *The new Party Programme*

Although the new Party Programme incorporates some important new positions on war and peace absent from earlier Programmes – in particular, the unwinnability of nuclear war and the concept of 'global problems' – its assessment of the prospects for peace remains within the traditional framework.[7] The outlook is uncertain and rather pessimistic.

The Programme warns that capitalism 'is still strong and dangerous'. This at least implies that capitalism should become less dangerous as it grows weaker. However, the remark that 'imperial-ism does not wish to reckon with the political realities of the contemporary world' is unaccompanied by any assurance that it will have to learn to reckon with them. Quite the contrary: 'The more powerfully the course of historical development undermines the positions of imperialism, the more hostile to the interests of the peoples becomes the policy of its most reactionary forces.' The implication here is ambiguous, depending upon the expected relative strength of the positions of the 'most reactionary' and 'less reactionary' forces within the imperialist camp – a matter left unclear. If the most reactionary forces are expected to remain dominant, the argument is suggestive of the confrontation perspective.

It is, to be sure, reaffirmed that war is not inevitable, for powerful forces are working to counteract the forces of war: 'Never has there been such terrible danger hanging over humanity. But never have there been such real possibilities of preserving and strengthening peace.' On the other hand, the conventional Leninist description of imperialism as 'parasitic, decaying and dying capitalism', incapable of overcoming its contradictions by reform, bodes ill for the demilitarization of East-West relations. The sense of the analysis taken as a whole arguably comes closest to the uncertainty of the fluctuation perspectives.

There is a striking discontinuity between the two sections of the Programme which deal with questions of war and peace. In Section III of the Third Part ('Relations with capitalist countries. The struggle for a stable peace and for disarmament.') the Soviet proposals for detente and international security are set out and urgently advocated. The tenor of the section devoted to theoretical analysis of 'the struggle between the forces of progress and reaction in the contemporary world' (Section II of the First Part), on which the discussion above is based, is suggested by the fact that the word 'detente' nowhere occurs in it.

A Party Programme to a large extent embodies a consensus of the most influential actors in the Soviet political system. The lack of clarity and coherence in this Programme is indicative of the prevailing ideological confusion.

(d) Statements by top foreign-policy figures

We have seen that the theme of interdependence occupies a prominent place in *Gorbachev*'s speeches, and that even in dealing with the correlation of forces he stresses its non-military dimensions. Gorbachev does not express the new ideological tendency in its most radical and consistent form, but it is his ultimate patronage of the general effort for ideological renewal which makes it possible for others at a lower level to do so.

Gorbachev's two most important appointees to the foreign-policy leadership – Foreign Minister *Shevardnadze* and Central Committee Secretary *Dobrynin* – are associated with the new tendency more unequivocally than Gorbachev himself. Dobrynin has spoken more directly than any other leader about the need to revise foreign-policy ideology in a humanistic spirit, in accordance with the 'peace first, socialism later' strategy.

The other Gorbachev appointee to the Central Committee apparatus in a position to influence East-West relations, *Yakovlev*, is less closely identified with the new tendency. His outlook on the prospects for peace in the short or medium term, especially so far as relations with the USA are concerned, is distinctly pessimistic.[8]

Ligachev, the Second Secretary of the Central Committee, is the most powerful figure to have a political base that is independent of Gorbachev. While his primary duties concern Party organization and personnel, his authority as an ideologist extends to foreign as well as internal affairs, and he also chairs the Foreign Affairs Commission of the Supreme Soviet.

In internal affairs Ligachev has been identified as a relatively conservative counterweight to Gorbachev, no less committed to 'restructuring' than his colleague but anxious to impose more rigid limits on the reform process. His address on the anniversary of the October Revolution in November 1986 suggests that Ligachev may play a similar role in foreign affairs.[9] 'New thinking' and 'interdependence' figure among the main themes of the speech, but he balances them with stress upon the necessity of 'sharp ideological struggle', and explicitly links 'the strengthening of peace on earth' to 'the strengthening of the international positions' of the USSR, of its 'weight, influence and authority on the international arena'. Recognizing the priority of peace, he is concerned that this not lead to neglect of the struggle for social progress (see Chapter 6).

A restraining influence on the new tendency may be exercised not only by Ligachev but also by senior Central Committee officials remaining from the Brezhnev era, such as *Shakhnazarov* and *Zagladin*. Zagladin, first deputy head of the International Department under both Dobrynin and his predecessor Ponomarev, though his own man and the patron of globalistics, still writes within the framework of the 'correlation of forces' orthodoxy. Nor, finally, are the statements of Minister of Defence Marshal *Sokolov* and other top military figures deeply affected by the new ideological tendency.

Personnel appointments and institutional changes

The appointment of Anatoly Dobrynin, Ambassador to the USA since 1962, to head the International Department in March 1986 marks a significant change in the role of this department of the Central Committee. Under Ponomarev it was concerned mainly with relations with non-ruling Communist Parties; its remit now seems to cover East-West relations as a whole. An arms control section has been set up within it under Maj-Gen. Starodubov. It appears that Gorbachev wishes to go further, and create on the foundation of the International Department a supreme body for the supervision of foreign affairs in their economic and military, as well as their political, aspects directly under the Politburo – a kind of Soviet analogue to the US National Security Council.[10] Other members of the leadership have evidently so far held up this plan. However, even the reorganization which has been achieved represents a strengthening of central Party control over the foreign-policy establishment, which under Brezhnev had evolved into a series of semi-autonomous empires – Gromyko's Foreign Ministry, Ponomarev's International Department and Ustinov's Ministry of Defence.

One method used to break up the empires has been quite an extensive circulation of senior personnel among them, as well as the infusion of fresh blood from outside the foreign-policy establishment. Thus an official in the Georgian Party became Foreign Minister, while Foreign Ministry officials (Dobrynin, Kornienko, etc.) moved across to the International Department, to be joined by a General Staff officer (Starodubov). Some senior specialists from the foreign-affairs institutes of the Academy of Sciences, formerly kept on the periphery of the policy-making establishment proper, have been appointed to important posts in the Foreign Ministry. In particular, the arms control expert from the USA Institute, V. Petrovsky, now heads the International Organizations Department at the Ministry as a deputy foreign minister, and the economist I.D. Ivanov, since 1979 deputy director of the Institute of World Economy and International Relations, was in 1986 appointed head of a newly created International Economics Department.

All this has implications both for ideology and for policy. The establishment has become more heterogeneous in outlook at the same time as its organization has become more unified. The more critically minded people from the institutes are no longer held at arm's length. Ivanov, a thoroughgoing exponent of the new ideological tendency, is now in a position to influence Soviet policy in the direction of greater interdependence in the economic sphere.

Summary assessment

Analysis of texts and of shifts in personnel and institutions suggests that, after the uncertainty and confusion of the early 1980s which followed the breakdown of the orthodoxy of the 1970s, the contours of a coherent new foreign-policy ideology may now be emerging in the USSR. The thrust of the new approach is to elevate interdependence to the status of the main material foundation of peace, with correspondingly reduced stress on the need for further change in the correlation of forces to the advantage of socialism, thereby separating the struggles for peace and for socialism out as tasks belonging to two distinct successive phases.

The political status of the new approach has risen since Gorbachev's accession to power from that of a tolerated and largely implicit tendency on the fringes of the political establishment to that of a prominent and explicit orientation enjoying top-level support – most notably from Dobrynin, and less directly from Gorbachev. At the time of writing, however, it is not yet certain that 'the new thinking' has acquired a securely dominant position. Resistance to it comes not just from the remnants of the Brezhnevite bureaucracy, the ousting of which we can expect in time to be completed; the more thoroughgoing variants of the new thinking appear to be rejected also by the military and by a section of the Party ideologists, perhaps protected at the top by Ligachev.

It needs to be borne in mind that this assessment is being made during a period of rapid change within Soviet ideology. Thus the reliability of the new Party Programme as a guide to dominant positions is already a matter of doubt. Had it been adopted in February 1987 instead of in February 1986, it might well have carried a stronger imprint from the new thinking.

Allowance must also be made for the fact that new positions are not yet fully worked out. Perhaps all that is really settled is the basic recipe for new thinking: to revise Marxism-Leninism in accordance with the requirements of the nuclear age and of an increasingly integrated world. It is accordingly useful to distinguish this general striving for ideological renewal from particular elaborated variants of revised ideology. Gorbachev is undoubtedly the moving force behind the general renewal, yet his public positions are less innovative than those of the most consistent of the 'new thinkers'. From Gorbachev's speeches one gains the impression of a man whose ideas are open to a variety of influences,[11] and who is not particularly worried that some ideas may be inconsistent with others – an ideal leader for overseeing the creation of a more flexible ideology.

11

CONNECTIONS WITH POLICY

It is not the purpose of this paper to examine Soviet foreign policy as a whole. However, the ultimate test of the significance of ideological change does lie in the sphere of policy. It will therefore be useful to note some connections which can be traced between the rise of the new ideological tendency and recent Soviet initiatives in the fields of arms control, trade relations and international cooperation.

Arms control

Soviet arms control policy under Gorbachev has been marked by a series of concessions and gestures of restraint which have often surprised Western observers. This is especially so in the field of nuclear armaments where, besides the repeated shifts in negotiating positions, we have seen the USSR take such unilateral steps as its prolonged moratorium on nuclear testing and its decision not to follow suit when the USA exceeded the SALT 2 limits. Policy change in the field of conventional armaments has so far been less dramatic, though the Soviet stances on verification and confidence-building measures have become somewhat more cooperative. Speculation about forthcoming withdrawal of Soviet troops from Eastern Europe remains unconfirmed;[1] such moves are perhaps resisted by the Czech and East German regimes, anxious about internal political stability, as well as by cautious elements in the Soviet leadership.

Dobrynin has explained conciliatory moves by the USSR as manifestations of 'the new political thinking, [which] presupposes a new, qualitatively higher degree of flexibility in foreign policy, a readiness to agree to reasonable compromises with one's negotiating partners'.[2] In the nuclear age, Gorbachev told the 27th Congress, security can only be mutual or common security:

> The highest wisdom is not in caring exclusively about oneself, especially to the detriment of the other side. It is vital that all should feel equally secure, for the fears and anxieties of the nuclear age generate unpredictability in politics and concrete actions.

And he proceeded to promise that 'in the military sphere we intend to act in such a way as to give nobody grounds for fears, even imagined ones, about their security.'[3]

A certain cynicism as to the sincerity of Soviet professions of dedication to mutual security is naturally evoked by the suspicious circumstance that they have almost always been accompanied by examples of the unwisdom of the *West* insufficiently taking into account *Soviet* security concerns. Are there signs that the USSR is now more prepared to recognize the legitimacy of Western security concerns? We shall briefly consider three problems bearing on this question: (a) the allocation of responsibility in Soviet analyses of the arms race; (b) the attitude taken towards Western anxiety about the offensive conventional capability of Warsaw Pact forces in Europe; and (c) the attitude taken towards Western reluctance to eliminate nuclear weapons under conditions of continued conventional confrontation.

(a) The arms race – whose fault?

All Soviet writers place the *main* blame for the arms race on the West, and most place the *whole* blame there.[4] But between total self-righteousness and the taboo thesis of 'equal responsibility' there is some room for manoeuvre. As Pat Litherland has shown, there has arisen in recent years a school of arms control specialists in the foreign-affairs institutes of the Academy of Sciences who have contested the completely one-sided orthodox view. As they conceive of the arms race, the primary thrust comes from the West, but the USSR may make such 'errors' as responding with unnecessarily drastic countermeasures or 'overinsuring' against anticipated Western strategic developments.[5]

The critical specialists tend to interpret the arms race as the product of a self-perpetuating dynamic of technological competition, rather than in terms of a conscious long-term quest by the West for strategic superiority. Burlatsky observes that 'the dialectic of the arms race, [by which] nuclear might on one side automatically stimulates the growth of nuclear might on the other side, automatically increasing the danger facing both sides, ... is scarcely accessible to customary awareness and traditional thought'.[6] Gavrilov and Patrushev, describing the arms race as a chain reaction and 'an unmanageable, quasi-anonymous force', argue that the unpredictability of scientific discovery and the leapfrog pattern of technological development 'give rise on the opposing sides to a feeling of uncertainty concerning strategic plans and the real possibilities of qualitatively raising their military potential.' They conclude: 'In such an atmosphere, countermeasures unjustified by reality are almost inevitable, growing into new rounds of the arms race.'[7]

This picture of the arms race casts both sides to some degree in the role of victims of the 'quasi-anonymous force', to be criticized not for aggressive intentions but merely for failing to exercise the diplomatic skill needed to solve the shared problem of bringing the malign process under control. Only the new thinking can understand and unravel the pattern of interaction: the nuclear arms race is 'the absurd fruit of backward thinking', of which the West has no monopoly.[8]

The whole concept of the arms race as an impersonal dynamic is, however, rejected by military ideologists. Col. Professor Dmitriev, accusing 'some Marxist authors' of inconsistency and confusion, warns that the 'hawks' of imperialism present the nuclear threat as a phenomenon 'outside of politics' in order to deny their own responsibility.[9]

(b) The offensive conventional threat
In Europe the main threat that the West perceives to its security comes from the offensive capability and doctrine of Warsaw Pact conventional ground and air forces. The USSR has long denied the reality of this threat on two grounds. First, it has been claimed that although the force structures of the two sides are asymmetrical they add up to a rough overall balance. Second, while the offensive aspects of Soviet military doctrine are admitted to some minimal extent, it has been argued that these aspects should not be regarded

as a threat, since they pertain to the military-technical side of doctrine, the crucial political side being purely defensive in nature.

A sign that this attitude might be changing came in July 1986 when Gorbachev declared to President Mitterrand of France, who was visiting Moscow: 'Let us look at all this anew. In those forms of armaments of which the West has more, let it carry out corresponding reductions, and in those of which we have more, we without wavering shall eliminate the "surplus".'[10]

Gorbachev reaffirmed his support for reductions aimed at eliminating asymmetry in his address to the Moscow Peace Forum in February 1987. He proceeded to stress the importance of confidence-building measures 'to reduce, or even better completely exclude, the possibility of sudden attack', advocating as one such measure that 'the most dangerous offensive types of armaments ... be removed from the zone of contact'. When he adds that 'in this respect, of course, military doctrines must be strictly defensive in character', the context suggests that he may have in mind the military-technical as well as the political side of doctrine.[11]

Another indicator of change is the terminology used to specify the correct level of Soviet armaments. It was stated before the 27th Congress that 'everything necessary reliably to defend the homeland' is made available to the armed forces, a formula amounting in practice to *carte blanche*. The new formula, enshrined in the new Party Programme, is that the armed forces are maintained 'at the level which excludes the strategic superiority of imperialism'. This implies a definite upper limit to military requirements.[12]

Similarly, 'sufficiency' has become a key term. 'We shall not make a single step in excess of the demands of sensible, sufficient defence,' promises Gorbachev.[13] The slogan of 'sufficient defence' was floated unofficially as early as 1984 by the defence expert Viktor Girshfeld, who linked it with reduced reliance on offensive armaments and unilateral troop withdrawals.[14] 'Reasonable sufficiency' is used at the same time to define the optimal end-point of conventional disarmament, though according to Dobrynin further research is needed to determine its precise meaning.[15]

However, the difficulty of detecting any analogous shift in the positions taken by Soviet military men suggests serious opposition in military quarters to substantial concessions in the conventional sphere (in contrast to the nuclear sphere, where the military seem more ready to accept concessions). Thus Chief of Staff Marshal

Akhromeyev, at a press conference in March 1987, repeated the old position that, given a rough overall balance, asymmetries in force structures are not a problem, NATO's advantage in anti-tank weapons and bombers compensating for the Warsaw Pact's advantage in tanks and fighter-interceptors.[16] The military ideologist Professor Gen.-Lieut. Serebryannikov, while paying obeisance to the need for 'new thinking', warns of the need always to take full account of the absence of new thinking on the other side, and concludes with the conservative formula: 'Everything that serves the interests of the reliable defence of socialism at the same time assists the strengthening of peace.'[17]

In the past, the monopoly enjoyed by the military over military information, expertise and advice has minimized the practical effect of more conciliatory ideas originating elsewhere in the political system below the level of the top leadership. The first substantial dent in this monopoly has now been made by creating an arms control section within the International Department of the Central Committee. Dobrynin has called for 'fresh, more profound and wide-ranging studies' of issues relating to conventional as well as nuclear disarmament, including the interdependence both of offensive and defensive weapons and of nuclear and conventional ones. These studies, to be conducted by natural scientists and foreign-policy scholars, are to assist the formulation of the new, more flexible arms control policy.[18] Just how substantial and influential the new academic studies will prove to be remains to be seen. Will the researchers, for example, be granted access to Soviet military data? Nevertheless, the decisive role of the military in security decision-making cannot henceforth be automatically assumed.

(c) *Making the world safe for conventional war?*

Of course, much Soviet propaganda, now as in the past, paints a simplistic picture of nuclear weapons as an unmitigated evil, while caricaturing the Western opponents of their abolition as nuclear maniacs inspired by the most sinister of motives. However, recent treatment of the nuclear disarmament theme by such analysts as Georgy Arbatov and Henry Trofimenko of the USA Institute and the *Izvestiya* commentator Alexander Bovin, as well as by Gorbachev himself, is more complex and open-ended.

First of all, as Arbatov recognizes, although some of those in the West who doubt the desirability of nuclear disarmament may be hypocrites concealing aggressive motives, 'it is important to see that for many the reason is sincere illusions'[19] – that is, they overestimate the reliability of nuclear deterrence, and fail to perceive the possibility of adequate substitutes for it. Bovin informs us that 'sceptics' who fear making the world safe for conventional war are to be found in the USSR as well as in the West.[20]

The analysts all grant that the existence of nuclear weapons does 'impose caution on the great powers and deter war'.[21] They all immediately add, however, that nuclear deterrence is not completely reliable, and that the risk of its failure cannot be tolerated indefinitely. Arbatov argues that nuclear war has so far been avoided largely thanks to chance: no leader of a nuclear power has made a big mistake during a crisis, nor has any crisis been complicated by internal convulsions. Nevertheless, good luck cannot be counted on as a guarantee.[22]

Moreover, the reliability of nuclear deterrence is expected to fall over the next two or three decades. The destabilizing effect of the technological arms race is usually mentioned in this regard, especially the potential for inadvertant war inherent in the trend towards automatic machine control of nuclear forces. Another fear is that Soviet-American nuclear parity may be superseded by 'a much more complex configuration of multipolar nuclear confrontation, the point of stable equilibrium of which could not be calculated by the "cleverest" computer'.[23]

Answers are more varied when we come to the question of what should replace nuclear deterrence. Fedor Burlatsky assumes that the function of deterrence in a world without nuclear weapons can be fulfilled by conventional armaments.[24] Arbatov and Trofimenko oppose reliance upon conventional deterrence, pointing to the catastrophic consequences of a conventional war in Europe – above all, the massive release of radiation which would result from attacks on nuclear power stations,[25] but also the pollution of the atmosphere from attacks on chemical factories, stocks of oil products and buried toxic wastes. 'Even conventional war would be totally destructive for human society'.[26]

The conclusion drawn is that not just a nuclear-free but a non-violent world is needed. In such a world, war would be deterred by 'the development of a system of multifaceted interdependence of States'.[27] Gorbachev too argues that the destruction of nuclear weapons does not mean returning to what preceded them. It is necessary that repudiation of nuclear deterrence not unbind the hands of military adventurers.

Some see the answer [to this problem] in the improvement of other components of military might, of conventional arma-ments. This is a mistaken path.

The correct path, he goes on, is to combine nuclear disarmament with the demilitarization and humanization of international rela-tions.[28] His target here is perhaps the advocates of conventional modernization within the Soviet military.

A glaring source of confusion in these discussions is the failure to coordinate the time-scales for the processes envisaged. It is urged that nuclear disarmament be completed by the year 2000. At the same time, it is not disputed that an effective substitute for nuclear deterrence is necessary. Conventional deterrence is felt to be unsatisfactory as a solution, but the alternative of a fully inter-dependent non-violent world is not claimed to be attainable within a decade or two. Given the rather modest arguments of Arbatov and Bovin to the effect that the feasibility of Gorbachev's disarmament programme is merely not to be excluded 'in principle',[29] one suspects that Soviet analysts really think in terms of a considerably longer time-scale, but are artificially constrained by the propaganda slogan about humanity entering the third millennium nuclear-free.

From propaganda statements one may gain the impression of a sharp divide between a Western establishment complacently attached to nuclear deterrence and a Soviet establishment obsessed with the nuclear threat but happy to make the world safe for conventional war. Closer study of the analyses of the more thought-ful people on both sides suggests that this stereotype is misleading. The main elements of the predicament – the need to prevent conventional as well as nuclear war, the less than total reliability of nuclear deterrence and the difficulty of finding adequate substitutes for it – are recognized in the USSR as they are in the West. To be sure, the stresses put on the various elements differ, but the basis for dialogue exists.

*   *   *

On balance, the new ideological tendency does appear to be associated with a shift in arms control policy in the direction of mutual security, though it is still too early to assess the full extent of the change. This may therefore be an opportune time for the West to facilitate the process by bringing forward its own arms control initiatives, designed to assuage the security concerns of both sides by linking the conventional and the nuclear spheres. Such an approach was tried unsuccessfully in the MBFR talks in the 1970s, when NATO offered to withdraw tactical nuclear weapons in return for the withdrawal of the 1st Guard Tank Army from East Germany.[30] There is reason to believe that it would now stand a better chance of success. The necessity of resolving the problems of conventional armaments and of tactical nuclear forces together as a single package has been advocated by Gorbachev himself, on grounds of the dual-purpose nature of the majority of tactical missiles.[31]

Trade relations
The theoretical debate on the 'all-world economy' (Chapter 8) foreshadowed radical changes in the organization of economic ties with the West. Reform legislation operative from January 1987 allowed selected enterprises and branch ministries to enter into direct relations with Western firms, breaking the monopoly of control over foreign trade long exercised by the Ministry of Foreign Trade. There soon followed a law making provision for the formation of jointly owned Soviet-foreign enterprises on Soviet soil. Soviet economists have advocated that the USSR and other European socialist countries take part in GATT as full members in order to facilitate economic relations between COMECON and the EEC.[32] Participation in the IMF and the World Bank is also said to be under consideration.

Particular efforts are being made to attract West European and Japanese firms into joint ventures. For example, the West German electronics firm Funk is setting up an international consortium to manufacture mass spectrometers and other high-technology products in the USSR.[33] Japanese business is being urged to invest in the development of Siberia on the basis of joint enterprise, with technological assistance to be paid for with raw materials. There are hopes for joint development of the Amur Basin border region with China.[34]

A definite decision seems to have been taken to abandon the traditional goal of autarky in favour of economic interdependence. The intensification of economic ties, as well as yielding economic benefits, is regarded as a means of enhancing security, especially in Asia.[35] There is a clear connection here between the ideological and the policy levels. The first soundings on the subject of Soviet-Japanese economic cooperation in Siberia took place between the Japanese Manufacturers' Association and the Institute of World Economy and International Relations in Moscow, where the ideological justification for economic interdependence was being elaborated.[36]

International cooperation

The USSR has already shown an increased readiness under Gorbachev to cooperate with the West on matters pertaining to 'global problems'. In the field of nuclear energy, for example, one might point to:

(a)   the international conventions for notification and mutual assistance in the event of a nuclear accident, and the enhanced role of the International Atomic Energy Agency, which followed the Chernobyl disaster (cooperation on the ecological problem);[37]

(b)   the agreement in March 1987 between the USSR, the USA, the EEC countries and Japan to conduct joint research towards building the world's first nuclear fusion reactor (cooperation on the energy problem);[38] and

(c)   the joint research of the USSR Academy of Sciences and the US Natural Resources Defense Council into methods of verifying nuclear test bans (cooperation on the security problem).

This last exercise illustrates a newly prominent type of cooperation, in which Western governments are bypassed and the USSR works directly with interested groups in Western society. During the Soviet moratorium, American seismologists, acting independently of their own government, had a listening post at the Soviet nuclear test range near Semipalatinsk.[39]

An important new example of direct cooperation between the USSR and Western scientists is the 'World Laboratory', to be financed through the 'Fund for the Survival of Humanity', the purpose of which is to bring together scientists from different countries to work on peaceful research programmes in a wide variety of fields (information science, earthquake prediction, education, fatal diseases, etc.). This venture, announced by Gorbachev at the Moscow Peace Forum in February 1987, is to be administered by an organizing group consisting of four Soviet representatives (not all scientists) and five scientists from the USA, West Germany, Japan and Pakistan.[40] The only Western country so far involved at governmental level is Italy.[41]

A more ambitious proposal for cooperation is the Soviet plan for the creation under the United Nations of a World Space Agency. This agency would coordinate and encourage the joint use of space technology for communications, navigation, remote geological probing, rescue, weather forecasting, production of new materials, space research and exploration. There would also be a global study of the state of the biosphere to work out measures for its preservation. Thus the preconditions would be created 'for turning terrestrial civilization into an interplanetary civilization from the very beginning of the third millennium'.[42]

We might also recall the proposal for a comprehensive system of international cooperation advocated by Burlatsky under the heading of 'the planning of world peace' (Chapter 5). This system is to comprise global programmes for the solution of all the global problems – a programme for the prevention of nuclear war, for disarmament, a demographic programme, an ecological programme and so on. The economic, social and educational programmes of UNESCO, though only partial or regional in scope, provide an initial model in miniature for the sort of planning needed.[43] 'The goal is step by step to strengthen the bases of robust, stable, long-term relations which could not be shaken by political conflicts spontaneously arising here and there.'[44]

Interpretation of the significance of the most far-reaching Soviet proposals for international cooperation presents problems analogous to those presented by the assessment of the most radical Soviet disarmament proposals. To the extent that recognition of the need for global cooperation is tempered by ideological pessimism concerning the ability of capitalism to participate effectively in it, the use of 'cooperation' as a propaganda theme may tend to substitute for the serious pursuit of cooperation in real life. Thus the plan for a world space programme is clearly devised as a propaganda response to SDI, an inspiring 'Star Peace' as the alternative to 'Star Wars'. One of the arguments used by Burlatsky against those who are sceptical about the feasibility of his proposals is that, even if 'planned peace' cannot be established for a long time to come, propaganda of the idea of planned peace 'in itself is already strengthening the influence of socialism' in the world.[45] The only sure way of resolving the persistent ambiguity of Soviet intentions is to test them out in practice.

12

IMPLICATIONS FOR THE WEST

The separation of the struggle for peace from the struggle for socialism by the new tendency of Soviet foreign-policy ideology implies that a settlement entailing a substantial demilitarization of East-West relations on terms that the West might find acceptable may become feasible over the coming decades. This admittedly involves some large assumptions: that the new tendency will consolidate its position and become a stable long-term influence over policy; that the West will perceive the opportunity and decide that it is in its interest to take it; and that the many complications on the way to a settlement can be resolved. Although the most radical disarmament goals may remain beyond the bounds of practical politics in the currently foreseeable future, it no longer seems so unrealistic to set the achievement of a significantly safer world as a medium-term goal.

The most likely objection is simply that Soviet claims of willingness to reduce the reliance of Soviet foreign policy upon military power are not credible. Ideological shifts which appear to buttress such claims must then be interpreted purely as the self-interested manipulation of Western opinion. The basic argument here is that only military power gives the USSR superpower status. The USSR is at such an irremediable disadvantage in all non-military spheres that the confinement of East-West rivalry to these spheres would put the USSR in a position of hopeless weakness. I shall argue that, on the contrary, it is not inconceivable that Soviet leaders might come to see substantial demilitarization of the East-West competition as being in their net interest, and so ideological change which appears to reflect this process merits careful analysis.

I turn next to more subtle misgivings. Some people may more or less accept my analysis of ideological change, but may nevertheless entertain doubts about whether the change is really in the interest of the West, at least in the longer term. Others may argue that it is a heightened military threat from the West that has brought about the shift to a less assertive Soviet ideology and policy, and that the threat must be maintained if the shift is to be preserved. Though Western policy-makers may be pleased that Soviet positions have changed for the better, they must prevent the process of demilitarization from going beyond a certain point; otherwise the USSR may revert to a more expansionist strategy.

But let us assume that the West should encourage and respond constructively to the new Soviet strategy. The problem remains that this strategy has not yet firmly established itself. We find ourselves on the threshold of a period in which the new thinking coexists with the old and reversal is a possibility. How is the transition period to be handled?

Finally, I consider how the West might assess and respond to the new Soviet strategy, on the assumption that it will come to guide Soviet policy. As the Soviet strategy combines cooperative elements, corresponding to interests common to East and West, with conflictual elements, corresponding to Soviet interests at odds with Western ones, I shall argue that an appropriate Western strategy of response must likewise combine cooperative with conflictual elements.

The credibility of demilitarization

The view that Soviet foreign policy must continue to rely predominantly on military power rests on two complementary propositions: that this has been and can be expected to remain a sufficiently effective and viable strategy; and that non-military strategies have been and can be expected to remain beyond the capabilities of the USSR. We have to make an informed guess at the present Soviet leaders' views of these matters, for it is their view and not ours which will mould Soviet policy. Here we must bear in mind that, even if the ageing Brezhnev leadership was content to get by from day to day, Gorbachev and his appointees have a time-horizon stretching into the next century.

It is undeniable that military power has frequently proven a valuable instrument of Soviet policy. It has also had some signal failures. Several years of fighting have not brought the war in Afghanistan any nearer to a successful conclusion, and when Soviet forces eventually do withdraw, there will be no guarantee of the survival of the client regime. On the global level, the collapse of detente and the heightened insecurity of the 1980s are the price paid by the USSR for its build-up and use of military power in the 1970s – an object lesson in the futility of the unilateral pursuit of security.

It is highly doubtful whether military strength and economic weakness can remain a viable combination for the indefinite future. As Philip Hanson has argued, the resources that the Soviet leadership can allocate to the military are constrained by irreducible minimum requirements of consumption (to ensure political stability) and of investment (to re-equip industry).[1] The constraints are bound to seem especially severe when it becomes evident how unrealistic were the high planned rates of economic growth that Gorbachev imposed over the objections of Gosplan officials. Moreover, volume of resources on its own is of limited assistance in competing with the West in high technology, increasingly important in 'conventional' as well as nuclear armaments. The military sector can only very incompletely be insulated from the deficiencies of the economy as a whole. Soviet leaders are well aware of these practical problems. They must also be aware that military power resting on a base of economic weakness is an anomaly from the point of view of Marxist theory.

The ability of the USSR to hold its own in political, economic and ideological competition with the West within a demilitarized international environment may well be doubted. But circumstances are conceivable in which the odds would not be stacked so heavily against the USSR – those, say, in which a Soviet society made somewhat more tolerable by internal reform and improved economic performance faced a West sunk in long-term depression and social disintegration. Perhaps only the most pessimistically inclined of Western observers would find this scenario plausible, but it is likely that dynamic and reformist Soviet leaders have more faith than we in the untapped potential of their own system and less faith than we in the socio-economic prospects of capitalism.

One of the proclaimed goals of internal restructuring is in fact that of restoring the ideological challenge presented to the West by the Soviet Union. 'If democracy develops in the USSR, if we succeed,' Gorbachev told a meeting of writers in July 1986, 'then we shall win.'[2] It is held that the West is afraid of reform and democratization in the USSR for precisely this reason, and has the unavowed goal of undermining them. In January 1987, a Soviet correspondent in Washington commented for the Moscow Home Service on American reaction to Gorbachev's reforms:

> They study and write so much about our reforms because
> they are afraid of them. That which hindered us and ...
> perverted socialism was to their advantage, because it made us
> weaker, more complacent, more inert, and because it alienated
> from the new world those who were prepared to search for
> other models, who could not fit in with the old world, who felt
> unhappy in it.[3]

Objections and misgivings

Some people perceive that an important shift is under way in Soviet foreign policy, but are wary of interpreting it in too optimistic a fashion. Their misgivings revolve around the danger of the eventual *reversal* of current policy changes, perhaps after some decades of a conciliatory approach. They interpret the shift not as the adoption of a new strategy for the indefinite future, but as the onset of a prolonged breathing-space in an unchanged long-term strategy of military aggrandizement – that is, as a tactic rather than as a strategy. Gorbachev realizes that the USSR has overreached itself and needs a period of retrenchment before it can resume its drive for world power. In this period the USSR, protected and assisted by good relations with the West, is to rebuild and modernize its economic base and tackle its internal problems. Meanwhile Western society, deluded into believing that the military threat from the USSR has permanently disappeared, loses the cohesion and determination necessary for an effective defence policy. Nuclear disarmament is completed, making the world once again safe for conventional war. At a certain point, the Soviet leadership concludes that the conciliatory approach has served its purpose and that conditions are ripe for the final assault on the West.

There are two possible variants of this interpretation. In the more Machiavellian version, both the adoption of the conciliatory approach and its later abandonment are planned in advance. In the more subtle version this assumption is not made, but it is argued that reversion to type would be the natural reaction of the Soviet political system to the amelioration of the unfavourable conditions which temporarily induced caution.

There are also two possible conclusions that might be drawn from such expectations for Western policy. A crude response would be to oppose frontally the new Soviet tactics and to maintain Western pressure upon the USSR unabated, in order to impede the strengthening of the Soviet economy and perhaps even with the hope of somehow bringing about the collapse of the Soviet system. On the other hand, awareness of the military and political risks of such a policy and of the unrealistic nature of the premises underlying the attempt to pursue the arms race as a tool of economic warfare might prompt a more sophisticated response. The turn in Soviet policy would then be cautiously welcomed, some arms-control and other agreements would be entered into in the interests of international stability and the management of public opinion, but pressure to push the process of disarmament beyond a certain point would be resisted as a hedge against the reversal of Soviet policy (as well as for other reasons). In particular, the abolition of strategic nuclear weapons would be rejected.

It is by no means obvious that fears of reversal are ungrounded. The history of Soviet foreign policy contains several sudden shifts of orientation, with an apparent tendency to alternate between uncompromising and conciliatory phases corresponding to periods of perceived Soviet strength and weakness. Thus the revolutionary optimism at the turn of the 1930s, when the West seemed fatally weakened by the Great Depression, gave way to the defensive united-front strategy of the mid-1930s when fascism came for a time to be seen as the main threat to Soviet security.

A Soviet commentator has alluded to the existence of some people who 'tend to believe that if peace is ensured the need for the new mentality will fall away and it will be safe to return to the old order of things'.[4] There are also the general points that the leaders of one-party States are better placed than those of pluralist democracies to impose unexpected changes of policy on their peoples, and to implement the rapid remilitarization of their economies.

100

However, the reversibility of Soviet policy should not be taken as an eternal given. As Soviet society becomes less isolated from the outside world, as the control of the power centre over social life gradually becomes less intense and as Soviet people come to take a more critical attitude towards public affairs, so must public opinion grow less malleable and the political risks and costs of an arbitrary shift towards an aggressive foreign policy become greater. Even the detente of the 1970s, though unaccompanied by any substantial internal relaxation of controls or demilitarization of society, has created some problems for the reimposition of a mood of high military vigilance in the 1980s, such as the 'pacifist tendencies' among parts of Soviet youth of which military ideologists complain. The impact of a lengthy period of simultaneous relaxation of internal and external tensions has yet to be tested. The growth of economic interdependence, which is an essential component of the new strategy, must also gradually act to constrain the scope for sudden about-faces in foreign policy which would endanger vital economic ties.

These processes are likely only slowly to make the new orientation of Soviet foreign policy less easy to reverse. It may take a long time for them to proceed so far as to pass the critical point beyond which reversal need no longer be considered a serious danger. Western analysts would need to make a continuous assessment of the reversibility of Soviet policy on the basis of study of Soviet society in all its political, economic, social and ideological aspects. It would be important to take these assessments into account in Western policy-making.

Finally, it might be remarked that not only the long-term political and economic reversibility of the new orientation of Soviet foreign policy is a matter of doubt, but also its ideological reversibility. The ideological justification of reversal would present difficulties, even if difficulties of this kind are rarely insuperable. The analogy drawn by Soviet historians between the united-front strategy of the 1930s and that of today is, after all, not an exact one. Fascism was an enemy which could be and was decisively defeated, and after its defeat the united-front strategy against it had no further purpose. The threat of nuclear war, on the other hand, can never be completely eliminated unless the knowledge of nuclear energy should somehow be irretrievably lost to humanity. Even after the abolition of nuclear weapons, international tension or conventional war could result in their re-creation and use. In *this* sense there can be now no 'post-nuclear age'. Thus a return to confrontation with the West would revive the nuclear threat which makes a conciliatory foreign policy ideologically necessary.

There remains the possibility that a citizen of the West, accepting the genuineness of the reorientation of Soviet foreign policy towards the demilitarization of East-West relations and not fearing reversal, might still oppose this development. Presumably the accusation flung by Soviet ideologists at Western 'militarists' – that they lack confidence in the ability of Western society to stand up to the USSR in peaceful competition – really does find its mark in such a person. His or her efforts might constructively be directed towards remedying the failings of Western society.

Managing the transition period

As was shown in Chapter 10, how to react to a consistently reoriented Soviet foreign policy may not be the problem immediately faced by the West. At present one observes rather an uneasy coexistence of 'old' and 'new' thinking in Soviet behaviour in the security field. Thus the repeated extensions of the moratorium on nuclear testing were impressive demonstrations of Gorbachev's determination to pursue security by political means. But nuclear testing was resumed just at the point when it appeared likely that the moratorium would finally bear fruit in the form of a successful motion in the US Congress to cut off funding for all but the tiniest American nuclear tests.[5]

A Western strategy to encourage the Soviet 'new diplomacy' would need to avoid both rigidity, which undermines it by making it seem futile, and readiness to make disproportionate concessions, which might undermine it by making it seem unnecessary. A policy of constructive and carefully graduated responsiveness might succeed in effectively linking Western responses to Soviet security concerns with more substantial Soviet responses to Western security concerns. For maximum effectiveness such an approach requires the support of the broadest possible public consensus. This would serve both to reassure the USSR that it need not greatly fear the return of the West to a confrontational stance, and to discourage it from speculating on the possibility that it might obtain significant unreciprocated concessions from the West.

If the new tendency in Soviet policy is to be encouraged, the West needs a heightened sensitivity to the nuances of internal controversy in Moscow, and to take them systematically into account in working out its own policy and negotiating strategy. For instance, Gorbachev has shown that he is willing to use summitry to make wide-ranging concessions capable of breaking through the stalemates caused by the cautious inflexibility of lower-level negotiators. Especially while pre-Gorbachev personnel remain in place, there will be great advantage in bringing issues which are proving sticking-points directly to the attention of the senior officials most closely associated with the new diplomacy, such as Dobrynin, Shevardnadze and Gorbachev himself.

The prominent role of the Soviet military in arms control negotiations poses a real problem in view of the limited extent to which they are influenced by the new thinking. Western politicians, diplomats and journalists may inadvertently help to shore up the internal status of the Soviet military by recognizing their pretensions to speak on behalf of the Soviet State. The greater military expertise of Soviet military men may make it more convenient to deal with them than with diplomats and Party officials, but preference should nevertheless wherever possible be given to contacts with people from the Ministry of Foreign Affairs and from the Central Committee apparatus. Otherwise the pressure on the Soviet military to share their expertise with their civilian colleagues is unnecessarily reduced.

Principles of a Western strategy of response

The new Soviet foreign-policy ideology recognizes that East-West relations are not a zero-sum game, that they involve converging as well as opposing interests, cooperation as well as struggle. At the present stage, indeed, shared interests and cooperation, both in the sphere of security and other global problems and in that of economic development, have priority over opposed interests and struggle. At a later stage, when progress in all these areas has at least taken the edge off the urgency of today's problems, the emphasis might be expected to shift back to opposed interests and the struggle between socialism and capitalism, though conducted in a safer, substantially demilitarized environment.

A complex Soviet strategy requires a correspondingly complex strategy of response from the West, similarly attuned to the simultaneous pursuit of shared and of opposed interests. East-West relations will become an increasingly dense web of interpenetrating cooperation and contestation. The West should not be deterred from cooperation for worthwhile purposes – say, to regulate the use of scarce non-renewable resources – by the natural tendency of the USSR to try to mould such cooperation into a Soviet-type model of global management. Instead, the West needs to counterpose to the Soviet model its own alternative model of market regulation, so that cooperation can evolve on a mutually acceptable basis.

As for the final outcome of the struggle, I see no reason to assume that it would amount to a clear-cut victory for one or another existing system, especially since demilitarization is likely in the long term to entail further blurring of divisions between the systems and the emergence of a world which, interconnected in some vital ways, would grow increasingly heterogeneous in others. When we consider that the economy of the USSR will very soon fall behind that of Japan alone, and within a few years may fall behind that of West Germany as well, fears that we are heading for a Soviet-dominated world seem far-fetched. Soviet strategy may be well-conceived and subtle, but it has no magical powers.

Paradoxically, the Western strategy most conducive to the expansion of Soviet power in the world might be that of ignoring or rejecting Soviet overtures for cooperation. The USSR would then become, by Western default, the main standard-bearer for 'all-human values' and the salvation of humanity from the various catastrophes threatening it. Conditions would be optimal for building up a broad united front of 'enlightened' world opinion looking to Moscow as its centre. Cooperation would expand anyway, but within the framework of institutions predominantly under Soviet influence. Some institutions of this kind have already been created under Gorbachev, such as the World Laboratory and its Fund for the Survival of Humanity (Chapter 11) or the 'Issyk-Kul Forum', a meeting-point for the world's writers established on the initiative of the Soviet Kirgiz writer Chingiz Aitmatov.

The political capital accumulated during the first stage of the Soviet strategy, the 'struggle for peace and cooperation', can later on be put to good use in the second stage, 'the struggle for socialism' (as the fruits of the united-front struggle against fascism were gathered in the aftermath of the Second World War). Dobrynin has urged Western communists to realize that by appealing to general human, rather than to specifically working-class or socialist, interests and values, they will 'open up new opportunities for expanding the influence of (communist) organizations over the life and strivings of the whole of society', transforming them from narrow class into broad national forces.[6]

The Soviet strategy is adapted in advance to any Western response. The West can only influence the relative duration of its two stages. By acting decisively to wrest the initiative from the USSR in the spheres of security and cooperation, the West can shorten the first stage, so that the USSR enters the second stage still in a state of relative political weakness. But if the first stage is painfully prolonged as Western governments appear casually to brush aside all appeals broadcast by the USSR in the name of humanity, then the USSR will eventually face the second stage from a position of real political strength.

As an economic power the USSR is falling behind. As a military power it has limits which its leaders are learning. Nor has the USSR for a long time been able, by pointing to the attractions of its own internal life, to hold its own as an ideological power. The only role in which it stands an immediate chance of competing successfully with the West is that of tribune for human survival in the nuclear age. The new Soviet strategy cannot be evaded; it can only be met.

NOTES

Only short references are given to Soviet articles, except for the most significant of the works cited, a list of the full titles of which follows the notes. All translations of extracts are my own. 'M.' indicates Moscow as the place of publication. The following abbreviations are used for names of journals:

KVS	Kommunist Vooruzhennykh Sil (Communist of the Armed Forces
KZ	Krasnaya zvezda (Red Star)
LG	Literaturnaya gazeta (Literary Gazette)
MEMO	Mirovaya ekonomika i mezhdunarodnye otnosheniya (World Economy and International Relations)
RKiSM	Rabochii klass i sovremennyi mir (The Working Class and the Contemporary World)
VF	Voprosy filosofii (Questions of Philosophy)

Chapter 1

1 D.K. Simes, 'The politics of defense in the Soviet Union: Brezhnev's era', in J. Valenta and W.C. Potter (eds.), *Soviet Decisionmaking for National Security* (London: George Allen & Unwin, 1984).

2 For a useful discussion of the interaction of ideological debate with the formulation of foreign policy, see Jerry F. Hough, *The Struggle for the Third World: Soviet Debates and American Options* (Washington, DC: The Brookings Institution, 1986), Chapters 2 and 9.

3 Arkady N. Shevchenko, *Breaking with Moscow* (London: Jonathan Cape, 1985), pp. 104–5, 180, 190, 280–1.

4   We might also note that the most combative passages are edited out
    of articles by Soviet ideologists when they are translated for use in
    publications aimed at a Western audience.
5   For example, the December 1982 issue of the Soviet journal
    Questions of Philosophy, devoted to questions of war and peace,
    contains both a highly conciliatory article by Burlatsky and some
    very harsh articles by military ideologists. A subscriber to all the
    English-language Soviet journals made available in the West
    (*Twentieth Century and Peace, Soviet Military Review, Socialism:
    Theory and Practice*, the English-language edition of *Moscow News*,
    etc.) will encounter a fair variety of Soviet views.

Chapter 2

1   Speech to the 1987 Moscow Peace Forum (*Supplement to 'Moscow
    News'* 1987, no. 8 (3256), p. 2).
2   The expression is that of the prominent historian V.G.
    Trukhanovsky (*Voprosy istorii* 1986, no. 10, p. 13).
3   For other recent accounts, see Raymond L. Garthoff, *Detente and
    Confrontation: American-Soviet Relations from Nixon to Reagan*
    (Washington, DC: The Brookings Institution, 1985), pp. 777–85, and
    T. Hasegawa, 'Soviets on nuclear war-fighting', *Problems of
    Communism* July-Aug. 1986, pp. 68–79.
4   'A new world war ... with present-day weapons means the
    destruction of world civilization' (*Pravda* 13.3.54). A similar
    statement was first made by the Central Committee Secretary
    Pospelov (*Pravda* 22.1.54).
5   *Kommunist* 1955, no. 4, p. 12.
6   Declaration of the Soviet Government, 21.9.63. For an account of
    Soviet positions in the 1950s, see H. Dinerstein, *War and the Soviet
    Union: Nuclear Weapons and the Revolution in Soviet Military and
    Political Thinking* (Atlantic Books, 1959).
7   *Pravda* 6.11.67.
8   E.g.: *Pravda* 22.7.74 and 24.6.81.
9   A. Krylov, *VF* 1968, no. 3, p. 3.
10 K. Bochkarev, *Voennaya mysl'* 1968, no. 9, p. 1.
11 Ilya Zemtsov, 'Sociology in the grip of politics', *Crossroads*, Spring
    1980. Zemtsov was a member of the editorial board of the
    information bulletin of the Soviet Sociological Association. He now
    lives in Israel.
12 Ogarkov here argued that there were 'objective possibilities of
    attaining victory', which may or may not be realized (*Sovetskaya
    voennaya entsiklopediya*, t. 7, M. 1979, p.555).

13 J. Somerville (ed.), *Soviet Marxism and Nuclear War: An International Debate* (London: Aldwych Press, 1981), pp. 31–2.

14 *Pravda* 12.7.82.

15 'Programma ...' (1986). The difference between the old and the new Programmes is noted by Ye. A. Zhdanov and V.P. Okeanov (*VF* 1986, no. 4, p. 8).

16 Statement on Soviet television, 18.8.86, p. 168, in M. Gorbachev, *The Moratorium: Selected Speeches and Statements by the General Secretary of the CPSU Central Committee on the Problem of Ending Nuclear Tests (Jan.-Sep. 1986)* (M.: Novosti, 1986). See also S. Shenfield, 'Nuclear Winter and the USSR', *Millennium*, vol. 15, no. 2, Summer 1986, pp. 197–208, and no. 3, Winter 1986, p. 415.

17 Meeting with scientists, p. 149, in Gorbachev, *op. cit.*

18 E.g.: Gareyev (1985), p. 417.

19 Trofimenko (1987). For another allusion, see the interview with Academician Moiseyev in *XX Century and Peace* 1986, no. 7, p. 18.

20 Bovin (1986).

21 E.g.: Gen.-Maj. Sushko and Maj. Kondratkov, *KVS* 1964, no. 2, p. 14; Maj.-Gen. Milovidov, *Voennaya mysl'* 1971, no. 11, p. 1. Admiral Shelyag said in 1973: 'I share most views on the global danger of [nuclear war] with the exception of the extreme views on the final end of civilization' (Somerville, *op. cit.*, p. 122).

22 *ibid.*, p. 124.

23 Yu. Ya. Kirshin and V.M. Popov, *VF* 1986, no. 2, p. 16.

24 Bochkarev, *op. cit.*

25 *ibid.*

26 Lieut.-Col. Ye. Rybkin, *KVS* 1965, no. 17, p. 50.

27 For further discussion of Soviet military doctrine as it relates to nuclear war, see J. Baylis and G. Segal (eds.), *Soviet Strategy* (London: Croom Helm, 1981), especially the essay by Benjamin Lambeth.

28 Moiseyev, *op. cit.*

29 'Colonel X's warning', *Detente* no. 1, Oct. 1984, pp. 2–3.

30 Gareyev (1985), p. 240. Similarly, Minister of Defence Marshal Sokolov writes: 'If used on a massive scale, [nuclear weapons] would destroy everything' (*KZ* 23.1.87).

31 E.g.: A. Bovin, 'Politics and war', p. 95, in *Peace and Disarmament: Academic Studies* (M., 1982).

32 *ibid.*

33 H. Kissinger, *Years of Upheaval* (New York and London: Weidenfeld & Nicolson, 1982), pp. 236–9.

34 E.g.: M. Cherednichenko, *Voennaya mysl'* 1973, no. 4, p. 47. For further discussion, see S.M. Meyer, *Soviet Theatre Nuclear Forces.*

Part I: Development of Doctrine and Objectives, Adelphi Papers 187 (London: International Institute for Strategic Studies, 1984), pp. 23–5, and A. Wohlstetter and R. Brody, 'Continuing control as a requirement for deterring', p. 142, in A.B. Carter, J.D. Steinbrunner and C.A. Zraket (eds.), *Managing Nuclear Operations* (Washington, DC: The Brookings Institution, 1987), pp. 153–63.

35 See Gareyev (1985); M. MccGwire, *Military Objectives in Soviet Foreign Policy* (Washington, DC: The Brookings Institution, 1987).

36 Trofimenko (1987); O. Moroz, *LG* 25.12.85, p. 12.

37 *Gubitel'nye posledstviya yadernoi voiny (sotsial'no-ekonomicheskie aspekty)* (M., 1984). The authors of the study are based at the Institute of World Economy and International Relations.

38 Some 1000 people were questioned about nuclear war by Moscow sociologists in February 1987 (*Soviet Weekly* 28.2.87, p. 7). 88 per cent denied and 4 per cent affirmed the feasibility of limited nuclear war, which suggests that those respondents who thought victory possible envisaged limited nuclear war.

39 A. Orkin, 'Soviet physicians against nuclear war: a PR ploy?', *Canadian Medical Association Journal* 15.2.84.

Chapter 3

1 Interview, *Detente* no. 8, Winter 1987, pp. 2–4.

2 Shakhnazarov (1983), p. 143.

3 G. Ye. Glezerman, *Zakony obshchestvennogo razvitiya: ikh kharakter i ispol'zovanie* (M., 1979), p. 69.

4 *Filosofskie problemy istoricheskoi nauki* (M., 1969), p. 74.

5 Eero Loone, *Contemporary Philosophy of History* (M., 1980), pp. 234, 260. Soviet discussions concerning the multilinearity of development of pre-industrial societies are examined by Jerry P. Hough, *The Struggle for the Third World: Soviet Debates and American Options* (Washington, DC.: The Brookings Institution, 1986), Chapter 3. For a fuller account of the Soviet philosophy of history, see James P. Scanlan, *Marxism in the USSR: A Critical Survey of Current Soviet Thought* (Ithaca and London: Cornell UP, 1985), Chapter 5.

6 Marshal N.I. Krylov, *Sovetskaya Rossiya* 30.8.69.

7 *Kommunist* 1955, no. 4, p. 12.

8 Interview, *op. cit.* Similarly, Shakhnazarov (1983) has written: 'A precondition of any rational prediction is the hypothesis which excludes the end of the world' (p. 726; see also pp. 30–1).

9 Grigoryan (1982). See also Grigoryan's first chapter in *Problemy. . .* (1983) and the review of this book by Mark Reitman, *Detente* no. 2, Jan. 1985, p. 18.

10   On Kant see I. Andreyeva and A. Gulyga, *LG* 28.1.87, p. 14. On
     Tolstoy see L. Saraskina, *XX Century and Peace*, 1986, no. 10, p. 42.
     Vernadsky's warning that Man would soon get hold of atomic
     energy and might use it for self-destruction, made in 1922, was
     quoted by Gorbachev in his speech to the Moscow Peace Forum
     (*Supplement to 'Moscow News'* 1987, no. 8, (3256)).
11   E.g.: Burlatsky (1982).
12   N.K. Krupskaya, *O Lenine*, (M., 1960), pp. 40–1, as cited for
     example by V.G. Trukhanovsky in *Voprosy istorii* 1986, no. 10,
     p. 14.
13   *Pravda* 25.5.86.
14   *Karl Marx and Frederick Engels: Selected Works in One Volume*
     (Progress Publishers, Moscow, and Lawrence and Wishart, London,
     1968), p. 35.
15   V. Zagladin, pp. 39–40 in *Peace and Disarmament: Academic Studies*
     (M., 1982), taken from Luxemburg's *Junius Pamphlet*.
16   Interview, *op. cit.*
17   S. Gerasimov, *LG* 2.5.84.

Chapter 4

1   C.N. Donnelly, *Heirs of Clausewitz: Change and Continuity in the
     Soviet War Machine* (Institute for European Defence and Strategic
     Studies, 1985), p. 22.
2   See, for example, the approving account of the work of the
     International Atomic Energy Agency by V.N. Misharin, *Sovetskoe
     gosudarstvo i pravo* 1982, no. 7, p. 38; and that of the UNESCO
     Energy Programme by B.M. Berkovsky and V.A. Kuz'minov,
     Energiya 1986, no. 11, p. 18.
3   *Pravda* 15.2.76.
4   N.M. Nikol'sky and A.V. Grishin, *Nauchno-tekhnicheskii progress i
     mezhdunarodnye otnosheniya* (M., 1978), pp. 71–3.
5   A.S. Milovidov and Ye. A. Zhdanov, *VF* 1980, no. 10, p. 32.
6   Shakhnazarov (1983), pp. 331–2; Milovidov and Zhdanov, *op. cit.*
7   V.P. Filatov, *Problemy kommunisticheskogo dvizheniya* (M.,1982),
     p. 19.
8   *ibid.*
9   Shakhnazarov (1983), p. 318.
10   In January 1977, at Tula, Brezhnev first declared that Soviet policy
     was 'not aimed at superiority in armaments' (*Pravda* 19.1.77). This
     has been repeatedly confirmed by Brezhnev and his successors.
11   Shakhnazarov (1983), pp. 143, 322.
12   Nikol'sky and Grishin, *op. cit.*, pp. 234–7.

13 Milovidov and Zhdanov, *op. cit.*; Filatov, *op. cit.*
14 Shakhnazarov (1983), p. 316.
15 Academician P.N. Fedoseyev, 'Technology, peace and contemporary Marxism', p. 17, in J. Somerville (ed.), *Soviet Marxism and Nuclear War: An International Debate* (London: Aldwych Press, 1981), pp. 23–5. This point comes last in a list of five factors underlying detente given by Fedoseyev, the first four being various aspects of the changing correlation of forces.
16 See Peter M.E. Volten, *Brezhnev's Peace Program: A Study of Soviet Domestic Political Process and Power* (Boulder, Co.: Westview Press, 1982), Chapter 4.
17 Shakhnazarov (1983), p. 317.
18 *ibid.*, p. 317.
19 *ibid.*, p. 318.
20 *ibid.*, pp. 396, 727–8.
21 V.V. Kosolapov, *Sotsializm i kapitalizm: nauka . tekhnika . proizvodstvo – sistemnyi analiz tendentsii i perspektiv razvitiya* (Kiev, 1983), pp. 162–5.
22 Arkady N. Shevchenko, *Breaking with Moscow* (London: Jonathan Cape, 1985), p. 285.

Chapter 5

1 Shakhnazarov (1983), p. 317.
2 A. Arbatov, *Voenno-strategicheskii paritet i politika SShA* (M., 1984), pp. 148–50.
3 G.A. Trofimenko, *SShA* 1980, no. 12, p. 52.
4 V.O. Pechatnov, *SShA* 1980, no. 12, p. 47.
5 V.V. Zhurkin, *SShA* 1981, no. 11, p. 4.
6 A. Bovin, *The Observer* 24.4.83.
7 G. Arbatov, *The Dream World of American Policy* (M.: Novosti, 1982).
8 A. Yakovlev, *MEMO* 1984, no. 1, p. 1.
9 A. Arbatov, *op. cit.*, p. 305.
10 G.A. Trofimenko, *SShA* 1981, no. 7, p. 3.
11 A. Yakovlev, *Izvestiya* 7.10.83.
12 A. Yakovlev, *Twentieth Century and Peace* 1985, no. 2, p. 24.
13 Zagladin (1984); Zagladin, *KVS* 1987, no. 1, p. 9.
14 G.A. Arbatov and W. Oltmans, *Cold War or Detente? The Soviet Viewpoint* (London: Zed Books, 1983), p. 5.
15 A. Bovin, *Izvestiya* 16.11.83.
16 Conversation with researchers of the USA Institute.
17 Yu. Krasin, *Social Sciences* vol. 12, no. 3, 1981, p. 81.

18 *Kommunist* 1984, no. 2, p. 4.
19 *VF* 1984, no. 1, p. 13.
20 V.I. Lenin, *Pol. sobr. soch.* t. 40 str. 244.
21 A. Prokhanov, *LG* 6.11.85; published in English in *Detente* no. 6, Spring 1986, pp. 16–8.
22 A. Prokhanov, *Pravda* 28.2.87.
23 Interview with R. Kosolapov, *LG* 1.2.84.
24 A. Krivitsky, *LG* 7.3.84.
25 F. Burlatsky, *LG* 4.1.84.
26 Gareyev (1985), p. 395.
27 *ibid.*, p. 437.
28 Grigoryan (1982).
29 Tomashevsky and Lukov (1985).
30 Krasin (1986).
31 See F. Burlatsky, *Planning of World Peace: Utopia or Reality?* (M., 1970; UNESCO, 1971).
32 Shakhnazarov (1983), p. 445 fn.
33 I. Mikhailov, *LG* 7.11.84.

Chapter 6

1 The historical record of Soviet caution in crises is surveyed by Hannes Adomeit, 'Soviet crisis prevention and management: Why and when do the Soviet leaders take risks?', *Orbis*, Spring 1986, pp. 42–64. For a less sanguine discussion of Soviet risk-taking, see Dennis Ross, 'Risk aversion in Soviet decisionmaking', pp 237–51, in J. Valenta and W.C. Potter (eds.), *Soviet Decisionmaking for National Security* (London: George Allen and Unwin, 1984).
2 S. Talbott (ed.), *Khrushchev Remembers. Vol. 2. The Last Testament* (Harmondsworth: Penguin Books, 1977), p. 557.
3 We know this from one of Dubcek's colleagues, Zdenek Mlynar, *Night Frost in Prague* (London: C. Hurst & Co., 1980), p. 241.
4 *Problemy kommunisticheskogo dvizheniya* (M., 1983), p. 134. This is the yearbook of the Institute of Social Sciences of the Central Committee, devoted to exchanges with foreign communists.
5 *VF* 1984, no. 1, p. 12.
6 Shakhnazarov (1983), especially pp. 309–10, 319; Shakhnazarov (1984).
7 Shakhnazarov (1983), p. 192.
8 *ibid.*, pp 234–5.
9 V.V. Kosolapov, *Sotsializm i kapitalizm nauka . tekhnika . proizvodstvo – sistemnyi analiz tendentsii i perspektiv razvitiya* (Kiev, 1983), pp 162–5.

10   The editor of the journal of Latin American studies summed up a
     discussion of revolutionary experience by observing that 'as yet only
     the armed path has led to the victory of revolutions in Latin
     America' (S.A. Mikoyan, *Latinskaya Amerika* 1980, no. 3, p. 35).
11   Mark N. Katz, *The Third World in Soviet Military Thought*
     (London: Croom Helm, 1982), pp 18–21, 38–9, 66–9, 97–8, 124–6.
12   Krasin (1986).
13   Dobrynin (1986b).
14   Plimak (1986). Plimak deals with the issue a second time in
     Politicheskoe samoobrazovanie 1987, no. 3, p. 66.
15   Serebryannikov (1987).
16   D.A. Volkogonov, *VF* 1985, no. 1, p. 26.
17   F. Burlatsky, *Planning of World Peace: Utopia or Reality?*
     (UNESCO, 1971). The paper was also produced in English in
     rotaprint by the Institute of Concrete Social Research, with which
     Burlatsky was then associated, for presentation at the 7th World
     Congress of Sociology, Varna, Bulgaria, in 1970.
18   Shakhnazarov (1983), p. 319.
19   F. Burlatsky, *LG* 5.10.83.
20   Articles entitled 'Filosofiya mira' in *Moskovskie novosti* 1.8.82; *VF*
     1982, no. 12, p. 57; and *Obshchestvennye nauki* 1986, no. 1, p. 56.
     See also the chapter by Burlatsky in *Problemy . . .* (1983), pp. 95–118.
21   Zhdanov (1987).
22   P.N. Fedoseyev, *VF* 1986, no. 5, p. 7.
23   V.V. Denisov, *VF* 1986, no. 5, pp. 90–2.
24   *LG* 5.11.86, p. 2.
25   *Pravda* 7.11.86. Gorbachev's statement was made on 20 October,
     Ligachev's on 6 November.
26   E.g.: Arbatov (1987) and Trofimenko (1987).
27   V.I. Lenin, *Pol. sobr. soch.*, t. 4, str. 220.
28   J.P. Scanlan, *Marxism in the USSR: A Critical Survey of Current
     Soviet Thought* (Ithaca and London: Cornell UP, 1985), Chapter 7.
29   Yuri Trifonov, *The House on the Embankment* (London: Abacus,
     1985), pp. 146–7.
30   S. Chuprinin, *LG* 25.3.87, p. 4.

Chapter 7

1   For relatively systematic expositions of the factors underlying the
    aggressiveness of imperialism, see: Shakhnazarov (1983), pp. 346–50;
    and M. A. Gareyev (1985), p. 436.
2   A. Yakovlev, *MEMO* 1984, no. 1, p. 1.

3   This is taken from a review (by E.P. Pletnev in *SShA* 1984, no. 2) of a book by a group of researchers at the USA Institute, *USA: Military Production and the Economy* (M., 1983).

4   *MEMO* 1986, no. 3, p. 132.

5   See A. James McAdams, *East Germany and Detente: Building Authority after the Wall* (Cambridge: CUP, 1985).

6   *Kommunist* 1986, no. 3, p. 83; *MEMO* 1986, no. 2, p. 28. Another proposal for revision of the draft to lay more stress on 'the influential wing of the bourgeoisie not connected with the military-industrial complex' was made by N. Zagladin, a lecturer at the Central Committee Academy of Social Sciences (*Kommunist* 1986, no. 1, p. 81). Academician Primakov, the new director of the Institute of World Economy and International Relations, has stated the Institute view that 'it would be incorrect to represent the US political superstructure' as homogeneously or permanently tied to the arms race (*LG* 5.2.86, p. 14).

7   Ivanov (1986).

8   Academician Primakov, in the interview cited at note 6, while defending the restricted conception of the military-industrial complex, rejects the debunking argument put forward by correspondent Vitaly Kobysh.

9   For some recent examples, see the book mentioned at note 3; V.P. Konobeyev and A.A. Konovalov, *SShA* 1982, no. 10; R.M. Entov, *SShA* 1984, nos. 1 and 2; Ye. V. Bugrov, *SShA* 1984, no. 3, p. 18.

10 S.M. Menshikov, who led this work, was appointed in 1970 head of a new Sector on Modelling Foreign Economies at the Institute of Economics and Organization of Industrial Production in Novosibirsk. He published an account of his input-output modelling of the US economy in *SShA* 1972, nos. 1 and 2. The political controversy to which the results gave rise is analysed by Vladimir G. Treml and Dimitri M. Gallik in Foreign Economic Report No. 2 of the Foreign Demographic Analysis Division of the US Department of Commerce (August 1973).

11 Ivanov (1986); see also I.D. Ivanov, *SShA* 1986, no. 2, p. 66. The same position is adopted, with greater reliance upon political as against economic arguments, by Krasin (1986).

12 Marx is quoted as saying that the national economy as a whole in no way needs 'to throw away a part of its capital into the water'. It is also recalled that Engels considered disarmament possible under capitalism. Lenin is harder to mobilize in the cause of 'the demilitarized model': Ivanov claims that 'while all-sidedly analysing militarism, Lenin did not include it among the basic indicators of

imperialism'. Page references are very sensibly cited only for Marx and Engels.

13 Col. S.D. Petrov, *Voenno-istoricheskii zhurnal* 1987, no. 3, p. 80.

14 V. Zagladin, *KVS* 1987, no. 1, p. 9.

15 M. Agursky, *Sovetskii golem* (London: Overseas Publications Interchange Ltd, 1983), p. 64.

16 R. Bykov and K. Lopushansky, *Nauka i religiya* 1986, no. 1, p. 41. For further discussion, see S. Shenfield, 'The militarisation of space through Soviet eyes', in S. Kirby and G. Robson (eds.), *The Militarisation of Space* (Brighton: Wheatsheaf Books, 1987).

17 *Obostrenie ideologicheskoi bor'by na mirovoi arene i politicheskoe vospitanie trudyashchikhsya* (M., 1983), p. 9.

18 Gareyev (1985), p. 436.

19 A. Grigorev, *MEMO* 1984, no. 1, p. 68.

20 A.A. Arbatov and A.F. Shakai, *Obostrenie syrevoi problemy i mezhdunarodnye otnosheniya* (M., 1981), pp. 213–15.

21 Arbatov (1987).

22 A.V. Nikiforov, *SShA i razvivayushchiesya strany: kritika kontseptsii 'vzaimozavisimosti'* (M., 1984), pp. 117–18.

23 Shakhnazarov (1983), pp. 191–3.

24 S. Tyushkevich, *KVS* 1981, no. 13, p. 75.

25 V.V. Kortunov, *Strategiya mira protiv yadernogo bezumiya* (M., 1984), p. 136.

26 Ivanov (1986).

27 I.D. Ivanov, *SShA* 1986, no. 2, p. 77.

28 Gavrilov and Patrushev (1984).

29 Krasin (1986).

30 A. Leonidov, *Vooruzheniya - na slom!* (M., 1960), p. 57.

31 V. Granov, *Kommunist* 1961, no. 2, p. 121.

32 Yu. Kirshin, *VF* 1982, no. 12, p. 67.

33 Arbatov (1987).

34 Bovin (1986).

35 *Obostrenie . . .*, *op.cit.*

36 Gorbachev (1986), p. 19.

37 T.T. Timofeyev, *RKiSM* 1984, no. 1, p. 18.

38 Dobrynin (1986a).

39 This point, often neglected in Western analysis, is convincingly demonstrated by Frederic S. Burin, 'The Communist doctrine of the inevitability of war', *American Political Science Review*, vol. 57, no. 2, June 1963, p. 334.

40 Shakhnazarov, *op.cit.*

41 Bovin (1986).

42 See F. Griffiths, 'Origins of peaceful coexistence', *Survey*, no. 50, January 1964, p. 195.
43 Speech on the work of the Soviet delegation at the 15th Session of the UN General Assembly, *Pravda* 21.10.60.
44 E.g.: A. Butenko and V. Pchelin, *Kommunist* 1960, no. 12, p.6, who were concerned to refute the Maoist charge that belief in disarmament is 'a pacifist illusion'; N. V. Ogarkov, *Istoriya uchit bditel'nosti* (M., 1985), p. 85; Krasin (1986).
45 A. Bovin, 'Sovetskaya programma razoruzheniya', *Izvestiya* 10.1.87.
46 A.N. Shevchenko, *Breaking with Moscow* (London: Jonathan Cape, 1985), pp. 101–2.
47 S. Talbott (ed.), *Khrushchev Remembers. Vol. 2. The Last Testament* (Harmondsworth: Penguin Books, 1977), pp. 550, 607–8.
48 Shevchenko, *op.cit.*, pp. 162–3.
49 Shakhnazarov (1983), pp. 727–39.
50 Bovin, *op.cit.*
51 Ivanov (1986).
52 Krasin (1986).

Chapter 8

1 See, for example: Gorbachev (1986), p. 26; P.N. Fedoseyev, *VF* 1986, no. 5, p. 7.
2 Speech to the Moscow Peace Forum (*Supplement to 'Moscow News'* 1987, no. 8 (3256), p. 3).
3 V. Zagladin, *VF* 1981, no. 9, p. 17.
4 V. Zagladin, *VF* 1986, no. 2, p. 3.
5 N. Inozemtsev, *MEMO* 1981, no. 3, p. 4; *Global Problems of Our Age* (M.: Progress, 1984).
6 D.M. Gvishiani, *Ekonomika i matematicheskie metody* 1979, vol. 15, no. 2, p. 233.
7 G. Khozin, *Global'nye problemy sovremennosti: kritika burzhuaznykh kontseptsii* (M., 1982).
8 See V. Zagladin and I. Frolov, *Global'nye problemy sovremennosti: nauchnyi i sotsial'nyi aspekty* (M., 1981); I. Frolov, *Global Problems and the Future of Mankind* (M.: Progress, 1982); D. Gvishiani, *Marksistsko-Leninskaya kontseptsiya global'nykh problem sovremennosti* (M., 1985); and D. Gvishiani, *Obshchestvennye nauki* 1986, no. 3, p. 103.
9 V. Zagladin, *VF* 1986, no. 2, p. 3.
10 Zagladin (1986).
11 V. Zagladin, *VF* 1981, no. 9, p. 17.
12 See, for example: Shakhnazarov (1983), pp. 207–8, 428–9.

13   V. Zagladin, *VF* 1986, no. 2, p. 3.
14   See, for example: *Global Problems of Our Age, op. cit.*, p. 18; Yu. Krasin, *Social Sciences* 1981, no. 3, p. 81; Shakhnazarov (1983), pp. 207–8; Tomashevsky and Lukov (1985).
15   V. Zagladin, *VF* 1981, no. 9, p. 17.
16   *Soviet Weekly Supplement* no. 2358, 18.4.87.
17   I. Frolov, *MEMO* 1986, no. 8, p. 3. See also N.N. Moiseyev, *Kommunist* 1986, no. 12, p. 110.
18   V. Zagladin, *VF* 1986, no. 2, p. 3.
19   The most systematic analysis of the interaction of global problems is that of Gavrilov and Patrushev (1984).
20   A.D. Ursul, *Filosofskie nauki* 1987, no. 1, p. 43.
21   B.T. Grigoryan, pp. 17–18, in *Problemy . . .* (1983).
22   Krasin (1986).
23   Tomashevsky and Lukov (1985). The last quotation is taken from the English-language summary of the article (p. 158); the challenge to the class approach in the text itself is not quite so explicit.
24   *ibid.* Exactly the same passage appears in an article by Oleg Bykov, a deputy director of the Institute of World Economy and International Relations (*MEMO* 1983, no. 4, p. 3).
25   L. Mitrokhin, *VF* 1984, no. 11, p. 79; the same line of argument is developed by Tomashevsky and Lukov (1985).
26   O.N. Melikyan, *RKiSM* 1983, no. 6, p. 11.
27   Tomashevsky and Lukov (1985).
28   Yu. A. Zhilin, *RKiSM* 1984, no. 2, p. 9.
29   Dobrynin (1986a).
30   E.g.: Z.P. Yakhimovich, *Voprosy istorii* 1986, no. 6, p. 3.
31   G. Sorokin, *Voprosy ekonomiki* 1983, no. 5, p. 127. See also A. Shapiro, *MEMO* 1985, no. 3, p. 91.
32   E.g.: Yu. Shishkov, *MEMO* 1984, no. 8, p. 72; E. Pletnev, *MEMO* 1985, no. 7, p. 106.
33   Bunkina and Petrov (1986).
34   *ibid.*
35   F. Burlatsky, *Novyi mir* 1982, no. 4, p. 221.
36   Elizabeth K. Valkenier, *The Soviet Union and the Third World: An Economic Bind* (New York: Praeger, 1983), Chapters 2 and 3.
37   See, for another example, the proposals of Academician Alexandrov, President of the Academy of Sciences, for East-West cooperation in developing nuclear energy in the Third World (*Peace and Disarmament: Academic Studies*, M., 1982, p. 8).
38   Ivanov (1986).
39   Bunkina and Petrov (1986). The expression 'peaceful living-together' (*mirnoe sozhitel'stvo*) was used in the 1920s but rejected by Stalin (F.

Griffiths, *Survey* no. 50, Jan. 1964, p. 195). It is of interest to note its recent occasional revival as a more positive-sounding alternative to 'peaceful coexistence'.
40 *Problemy* ... (1983), p. 87.
41 *Kommunist* 1986, no. 3, p. 83; *MEMO* 1986, no. 2, p. 28.

Chapter 9
1 Gorbachev (1986). See especially pp. 7, 16, 26–7, 93–6.
2 The example cited by Shakhnazarov in his interview with Jeff Gleisner (*Detente* no. 8, Winter 1987).
3 Burlatsky (1982).
4 Gorbachev (1986), p. 24.
5 Bovin (1986); also in *Twentieth Century and Peace* 1986, no. 9, p. 6.
6 Zagladin (1986).
7 *Global Problems of Our Age* (M.: Progress, 1984), pp. 57–8.
8 *RKiSM* 1985, no. 2, p. 89.
9 Speech at the 18th Congress of the Soviet trade unions, 25 Feb. 1987, *Supplement to 'Moscow News'* 1987, no. 10 (3258), p.5.
10 *ibid.*; speech at meeting in Vladivostok on 28 July 1986 (M. Gorbachev, *The Moratorium*, M.: Novosti, 1986), p. 161.
11 Statement on Soviet television on 18 Aug. 1986 (Gorbachev, *op. cit.*, p. 173).
12 S. Talbott (ed.), *Khrushchev Remembers. Vol. 2. The Last Testament* (Harmondsworth: Penguin, 1977), p. 266.

Chapter 10
1 This selection, while no doubt not exhaustive, is unlikely to be grossly misleading. Where the same author makes similar points in a number of articles, only the first article to appear is included. The sixteen articles were: Grigoryan, *VF* 1982, no. 9, p. 36; Burlatsky, *VF* 1982, no. 12, p. 57; Bykov, *MEMO* 1983, no. 4, p. 3; Melikyan, *RKiSM* 1983, no. 6, p. 11; Gavrilov and Patrushev, *VF* 1984, no. 5, p. 99; Mitrokhin, *VF* 1984, no. 11, p. 79; Mikhailov, *LG* 7.11.84; Tomashevsky and Lukov, *MEMO* 1985, no. 4, p. 17; Krasin, *MEMO* 1986, no. 1, p. 3; Ivanov, *SShA* 1986, no. 2, p. 14; Yakhimovich, *Voprosy istorii KPSS* 1986, no. 6, p. 3; Bovin, *Kommunist* 1986, no. 10, p. 113; Plimak, *Pravda* 14.11.86; Arbatov, *Kommunist* 1987, no. 2, p. 104; Trofimenko, *SShA* 1987, no. 2, p. 3; and Zhdanov, *Pravda* 6.3.87.
2 Comparison of article by Krasin in note 1 with his article in *Obshchestvennye nauki* 1981, no. 3, p. 81.

3   M.I. Basmanov, *Kommunisty i mir* (*istoricheskii opyt i sovremennost'*) (M., 1986), pp. 19–20, 24, 118–20.
4   *Znamya* 1986, no. 1, p. 3.
5   The number of slogans was 83 in 1982, 61 in 1983, 63 in 1984, 44 in 1985 and 50 in 1986.
6   See *Pravda* 17.10.82; 16.10.83; 11.10.84; 13.10.85; 19.10.86. For the slogans in English, see *Current Digest of the Soviet Press*, vol. 34, no. 42; vol. 35, no. 42; vol. 36, no. 41; vol. 37, no. 42; vol. 38, no. 42.
7   'Programma . . .' (1986).
8   In his latest article, Yakovlev laments the enormous strength of the forces of war in the USA, 'a society suffering from a complex of being doomed' (*Kommunist* 1986, no. 17, p. 3).
9   Ye. K. Ligachev, speech on 6.11.86, *Pravda* 7.11.86, p. 3.
10 This is based on a briefing which Zagladin gave guests from West European Social-Democratic Parties during the 27th Party Congress.
11 One small illustration of this point. Commentators have been struck by the rhetorical questions posed by Gorbachev at his meeting with a group of Soviet writers on 19 June 1986: 'If not us, who? And if not now, when?' (P. Frank, 'Gorbachev and the "psychological restructuring" of Soviet society', *The World Today*, vol. 43, no. 5, May 1987, p. 85). Gorbachev is here paraphrasing a well-known Talmudic saying, attributed to Rabbi Hillel in the first century BC: 'If I am not for myself, who will be for me? . . . And if not now, when?' (Primo Levi, *If Not Now, When?*, London: Abacus, 1987, p. 280).

Chapter 11

1   Martin Walker, *The Guardian* 15.3.87, 12.4.87.
2   Dobrynin (1986b).
3   Gorbachev (1986), pp. 82, 85.
4   E.g.: 'No, not I, not my Party, not my people are guilty . . . Guilty are the black imperialist forces . . .' (A. Prokhanov, *Pravda* 28.2.87).
5   P. Litherland, *Gorbachev and Arms Control: Civilian Experts and Soviet Policy*, Peace Research Report No. 12 (School of Peace Studies, University of Bradford, Nov. 1986), Chapters 6–8.
6   Burlatsky (1982).
7   Gavrilov and Patrushev (1984). The sensitivity of explicit criticism of Soviet policy is shown by the fact that the phrase 'unjustified by reality' was deleted from two other published versions of this essay (Litherland, *op. cit.*, p.68).
8   A. Voznesensky, *Sovetskaya kultura* 21.2.87, p. 7.
9   Col. Prof. A. Dmitriev, *KVS* 1984, no. 5, p. 36.
10 *Pravda* 8.7.86.

11 *Supplement to 'Moscow News'* 1987, no. 8 (3256), p. 3. There have been reports in the media that Gorbachev has admitted the existence of 'disparity' between the forces of the two sides in Europe. This is a misleading translation; the term regularly used is the more neutral one of 'asymmetry'.

12 C. Glickham, *New Directions for Soviet Foreign Policy, Radio Liberty Research Bulletin, RL Supplement 2/86*, 6.9.86, pp. 15–6.

13 Speech at the 18th Congress of the Soviet trade unions, 25 Feb. 1987, *Supplement to 'Moscow News'* 1987, no. 10 (3258), p. 2.

14 S. Shenfield, 'The USSR: Viktor Girshfeld and the concept of "sufficient defence"', *ADIU Report* (University of Sussex), Jan.-Feb. 1984, p. 10.

15 Dobrynin (1986b).

16 Press conference on 2 March 1987, reported in *The Guardian* 3.3.87, p. 8.

17 Prof. Gen.-Lieut. V. Serebryannikov, *KZ* 19.12.86, pp. 2–3.

18 Dobrynin (1986b).

19 Arbatov (1987).

20 A. Bovin, *Izvestiya* 10.1.87.

21 Arbatov (1987).

22 *ibid.*

23 Trofimenko (1987).

24 F. Burlatsky, *LG* 29.1.86, p. 14.

25 Trofimenko (1987). He considers that this radiation on its own would mean the end of Europe.

26 Arbatov (1987).

27 N. Sokov, *XX Century and Peace* 1987, no. 3, p. 5.

28 Address to the Moscow Peace Forum, *Supplement to 'Moscow News'* 1987, no. 8 (3256).

29 Arbatov (1987), Bovin, *op. cit.*

30 See L. Ruehl, *MBFR: Lessons and Problems*, Adelphi Paper No. 176 (London: International Institute for Strategic Studies, 1982).

31 Speech at a rally in Prague, April 1987 (*Soviet Weekly Supplement* no. 2358, 18.4.87).

32 E.g.: *MEMO* 1986, no. 11, p. 124.

33 *Soviet Weekly* 21.2.87, p. 3.

34 See the interview on Asian security with Georgy Kim, a senior analyst at the Institute of Oriental Studies (*LG* 18.3.87, pp. 9, 14).

35 *ibid.*

36 I am indebted for this information to Professor Nobuo Shimotomai of Seikei University.

37 W. Patterson, 'Nuclear watchdog finds its role', *New Scientist* 23.4.87, p. 50.

38 *The Guardian* 18.3.87.
39 See the record of Gorbachev's meeting with representatives of the International Forum of Scientists for a Nuclear Test Ban, 14 July 1986, p. 139, in M. Gorbachev, *The Moratorium* (M.: Novosti, 1986).
40 *LG* 18.2.87, p. 2.
41 *Soviet Weekly* 14.3.87.
42 *Pravda* 13.6.86, p. 4 (*Current Digest of the Soviet Press*, vol. 38, no. 24, 16.7.86, pp. 15–16).
43 Burlatsky (1982).
44 *Problemy* . . . (1983), p. 117.
45 F. Burlatsky, *Obshchestvennye nauki* 1986, no. 1, p. 69.

Chapter 12

1 P. Hanson, 'Soviet economic problems? – an opportunity for progress in arms control', *Detente* no. 1, Oct. 1984, p. 4.
2 This speech is unpublished, but circulates in *samizdat*. For an English translation, see *Detente* no. 8, Winter 1987, p. 12.
3 Report from Washington, DC, by V. Dunayev, Moscow Home Service 14.1.87 (*SWB* SU/8471/A1/5–6, 21.1.87).
4 N. Sokov, *XX Century and Peace* 1987, no. 3, p. 5.
5 American scientists forcefully urged their Soviet colleagues at the Moscow Peace Forum in February 1987 that nuclear testing not be resumed before the motion had a chance to pass through the Congress (J. Leggett, *New Statesman* 27.2.87, p. 8). In fact, Soviet scientists were receptive to this appeal. Academician Velikhov, Vice-President of the Academy of Sciences and Gorbachev's science adviser, stated in a lecture to students at Moscow University in March 1987 that he thought that the moratorium could and should have been continued (*Moscow News* 1987, no. 15, 12.4.87, p. 6).
6 Dobrynin (1986a).

LIST OF THE
MOST SIGNIFICANT
SOVIET WORKS

Arbatov, G., 'Militarizm i sovremennoe obshchestvo', *Kommunist* 1987, no. 2, p. 113.

Bovin, A., 'Novoe myshlenie – trebovanie yadernogo veka', *Kommunist* 1986, no. 10, p. 113.

Bunkina, M., and N. Petrov, 'Vsemirnoe khozyaistvo – ekonomicheskii fundament mirnogo sosushchestvovaniya', *MEMO* 1986, no. 9, p. 49.

Burlatsky, F., 'Filosofiya mira', *VF* 1982, no. 12, p. 57.

Dobrynin, A.F., 'Glavnaya obshchestvennaya sila sovremennosti', *RKiSM* 1986a, no. 6, p. 9.

Dobrynin, A.F., 'Za bez'yadernyi mir, navstrechu XXI veku', *Kommunist* 1986b, no. 9, p. 18.

Gareyev, M.A., *M.V. Frunze – voennyi teoretik* (M., 1985).

Gavrilov, V.M., and S.V. Patrushev, 'Gonka vooruzhenii v ierarkhii global'nykh problem', *VF* 1984, no. 5, p. 99.

Gorbachev, M., *Political Report of the CPSU Central Committee to the 27th Party Congress* (M.: Novosti, 1986).

Grigoryan, B.T., 'Zakonomernost' i otkrytost' istorii v svete problemy voiny i mira', *VF* 1982, no. 9, p. 36.

Krasin, Yu., 'Strategiya mira – imperativ epokhi', *MEMO* 1986, no. 1, p. 3.

Ivanov, I.D., 'Amerikanskie korporatsii i militarizm', *SShA* 1986, no. 2, p. 14.

Plimak, Ye., 'Marksizm-Leninizm i revolyutsionnye perspektivy v kontse XX veka', *Pravda* 14.11.86. Problemy mira i sotsial'nogo progressa v sovremennoi filosofii (M., 1983).

'Programma Kommunisticheskoi Partii Sovetskogo Soyuza: Novaya redaktsiya', *Kommunist* 1986, no. 4, p. 131.

Serebryannikov, V., 'S uchetom real'nostei yadernogo veka', *KVS* 1987, no. 3, p. 9.

Shakhnazarov, G. Kh., *Sotsializm i budushchee* (M., 1983).

Shakhnazarov, G. Kh., 'Logika politicheskogo myshleniya v yadernuyu eru', *VF* 1984, no. 5, p. 68.

Tomashevsky, D., and V. Lukov, 'Interesy chelovechestva i mirovaya politika', *MEMO* 1985, no. 4, p. 17.

Trofimenko, G.A., 'Novye real'nosti i novoe myshlenie', *SShA* 1987, no. 2, p. 3.

Zagladin, V.V., 'Marksizm-Leninizm o roli rabochego klassa v mezhdunarodnykh otnosheniyakh', *RKiSM* 1984, no. 4, p. 15.

Zagladin, V.V., 'Sotsializm i global'nye problemy sovremennosti', *Politicheskoe samoobrazovanie* 1986, no. 9, p. 13.

Zhdanov, Yu., 'Klassovoe i obshchechelovecheskoe v yadernyivek', *Pravda* 6.3.87.

GLOSSARY OF THE MOST IMPORTANT SOVIET AUTHORS

AKHROMEYEV, Marshal S.F. – Chief of General Staff

ARBATOV, Aleksei G. – Head of department, Institute of World Economy and International Relations

ARBATOV, Academician Georgy A. – Director of the Institute for the Study of the USA and Canada

BOVIN, Alexander – Influential publicist; political observer for *Izvestiya*

BURLATSKY, Fedor M. – Political scientist and publicist; political observer for *Literaturnaya gazeta* (*The Literary Gazette*); head of Department of Philosophy, Central Committee Institute of Social Sciences

BYKOV, Oleg N. – Deputy Director of the Institute of World Economy and International Relations

DOBRYNIN, Anatoly F. – Secretary of the Central Committee, head of the International Department of the Central Committee; formerly Ambassador to the USA

FEDOSEYEV, Academician P.N. – Philosopher, Vice-President of the Academy of Sciences; formerly director of the Institute of Philosophy and of the Central Committee Institute of Marxism-Leninism

FROLOV, Academician I.T. – Philosopher, Chief Editor of *Kommunist*; Chairman of the Scientific Council of the Academy of Sciences on Philosophical and Social Problems of Science and Technology; formerly Chief Editor of *Voprosy filosofii* (*Questions of Philosophy*)

GAREYEV, Gen.-Col. M.A. – Deputy Chief of General Staff, head of the Military Science Directorate of the General Staff

GORBACHEV, M.S. – General Secretary of the Central Committee

GRIGORYAN, B.T. – Member of the Institute of Philosophy

GVISHINAI, Academician Jermen M. – First deputy chairman of Gosplan; director of the All-Union Scientific Research Institute for Systems

Investigations; chairman of the Council of the International Institute
for Applied Systems Analysis, Vienna; formerly deputy chairman of the
State Committee for Science and Technology

INOZEMTSEV, Academician N.N. – Former director of the Institute of
World Economy and International Relations (died 1982)

IVANOV, I.D. – Head of the new International Economics Department,
Ministry of Foreign Affairs; formerly Economic Affairs Officer at
UNCTAD (1966–71) and deputy director of the Institute of World
Economy and International Relations (1979–86)

KOSOLAPOV, R.I. – Former First Deputy Chief Editor of *Pravda* (1974–6)
and Chief Editor of *Kommunist* (1976–86); no longer prominent

KRASIN, Prof. Yuri – Philosopher, Pro-Rector of the Central Committee
Academy of Social Sciences

LIGACHEV, Ye. K. – Member of Politburo, Second Secretary of the
Central Committee, Chairman of the Foreign Affairs Commission of
the USSR Supreme Soviet

MALENKOV, G.M. – Chairman of the Council of Ministers (1953–5);
ousted from all positions as member of the 'anti-Party group' (1957)

MOISEYEV, Academician N.N. – Mathematical physicist and ecospheric
modeller, director of the Computer Centre of the Academy of Sciences

OGARKOV, Marshal N.V. – Head of the Western Theatre of Military
Operations; formerly Chief of General Staff

PLIMAK, Ye. – Historian and theorist of the revolutionary movement, at
the Institute of the International Workers' Movement; formerly at the
Institute of Philosophy

PRIMAKOV, Academician Ye. M. – Director of the Institute of World
Economy and International Relations; formerly director of the Institute
of Oriental Studies (1978–86)

RUSAKOV, K.V. – Formerly Secretary of the Central Committee and head
of the Central Committee Department for Liaison with Communist
and Workers' Parties of Socialist Countries

SHAKHNAZAROV, Prof. G. Kh. – Political scientist and official; Chairman
of the Soviet Political Science Association; First Deputy Head, Central
Committee Department for Liaison with Communist and Workers'
Parties of Socialist Countries

SHAPOSHNIKOV, V.S. – First Deputy Head, International Department of
the Central Committee

SHEVARDNADZE, E.A. – Minister of Foreign Affairs

SOKOLOV, Marshal S.L. – Minister of Defence

TIMOFEYEV, T.T. – Historian and economist, director of the Institute of
the International Workers' Movement

TROFIMENKO, G.A. – Head of the Department of US Foreign Policy,
Institute for the Study of the USA and Canada

USTINOV, Marshal D.F. – Late Minister of Defence

VOLKOGONOV, Gen.-Lieut. Prof. D.A. – Deputy Head of the Main
Political Administration of the Armed Forces

YAKOVLEV, Alexander N. – Secretary of the Central Committee, head of
the Propaganda Department of the Central Committee; formerly
Deputy Head of the Department of Science and Culture and of the
Department of Propaganda of the Central Committee (1965–73),
Ambassador to Canada (1973–83), director of the Institute of World
Economy and International Relations (1983–5)

ZAGLADIN, N.V. – Lecturer, Central Committee Academy of Social
Sciences

ZAGLADIN, Prof. Vadim V. – First Deputy Head of the International
Department of the Central Committee, with special responsibility for
Western Europe; disarmament spokesman

ZHILIN, Yuri A. – Head of group of consultants on foreign policy to the
Central Committee

Related forthcoming titles

The Soviet Union and Cuba
Peter Shearman

In the 1970s Soviet and Cuban activity in the Third World was perceived by some in the West as being responsible for undermining superpower détente. Furthermore, it has often been argued that Cuba acts as a surrogate of the USSR. In this paper the surrogate thesis is assessed by examining the Soviet-Cuban link in four revolutionary or conflict situations: Angola, Ethiopia, Grenada and Nicaragua. It is shown that Cuba is largely an autonomous actor in international relations, and that Western reaction to Cuban and Soviet activity in the Third World is therefore often based on misperceptions. The author points out the dangers of such misperceptions and suggests a more rational strategy for dealing with the 'Soviet-Cuban threat'.

Soviet Foreign Policy Priorities under Gorbachev
Alex Pravda

Gorbachev has clearly brought a more energetic and flexible style to the conduct of Soviet foreign policy, but has he altered its substance? This paper examines new elements in Soviet thinking about security and foreign policy priorities and the relative utility of military and political instruments in advancing them. It also assesses the effects of tightening domestic constraints and an increasingly difficult international environment. In order to gauge the extent of actual as distinct from declaratory shifts in priorities, the paper reviews recent policy towards the United States, Western Europe, the socialist bloc and major Asian states. Finally, it examines the policy implications of such shifts for the West in general and Western Europe in particular.

The Soviet Union and India
Peter Duncan

India is the only non-communist country in the Third World with which the Soviet Union has managed to maintain friendly relations over a prolonged period. To what extent is the closeness of India to the USSR on many foreign policy issues the result of a coincidence of interests rather than Soviet influence? This paper assesses the balance of costs and benefits to the USSR of its considerable economic and military involvement with India, and concludes by examining the implications of possible shifts in Soviet policy in the region for Western links with India.

Routledge & Kegan Paul